# THE ARMY
# OF THE FUTURE

General de Gaulle

# THE ARMY OF THE FUTURE

by

## GENERAL DE GAULLE

HUTCHINSON & CO. (Publishers) LTD.
LONDON AND MELBOURNE

MADE AND PRINTED IN GREAT BRITAIN
AT GAINSBOROUGH PRESS, ST. ALBANS,
BY FISHER, KNIGHT & CO., LTD.

# CONTENTS

# LIST OF ILLUSTRATIONS

## MAP

*"Old clay made for sorrow."*—ALBERT SAMAIN.

# PROTECTION

# I

AS LOOKING AT A PORTRAIT SUGGESTS THE IMPRESSION of the subject's destiny to the observer, so the map of France tells our own fortune. The body of the country has in its centre a citadel, a forbidding mass of age-old mountains, flanked by the tablelands of Provence, Limousin, and Burgundy ; and, all around, vast slopes, for the most part difficult of access to anyone attacking them from the outside and split by the gorges of the Saone, the Rhone and the Garonne, barred by the walls of the Jura Alps and the Pyrenees or else plunging in the distance into the English Channel, the Atlantic, or the Mediterranean ; but in the North-East, there is a terrible breach between the essential basins of the Seine and of the Loire and German territory. The Rhine, which nature meant the Gauls to have as their boundary and their protection, has hardly touched France before it leaves her and lays her open to attack.

It is true that the Vosges set up a wide rampart, but it is one which can be turned by the gap at Belfort or by the salt marshes. It is true that the slopes of the Moselle and those of the Meuse, resting at one end on the Lorraine tableland and at the other on the Ardennes, form appreciable but not very deep obstacles, which a slight error, surprise, or neglect would be sufficient to lose, and which would become vulnerable from the rear with the first withdrawal in Hainaut or in Flanders. For, in these low-lying plains, there is neither wall nor ditch upon which to

base resistance : there are no lines of dominating
heights, no rivers running parallel to the front. Worse
still, the lie of the land there appears specially designed
to facilitate invasion by multiple penetrating routes,
the valleys of the Meuse, of the Sambre, of the Scheldt,
of the Scarpe, and of the Lys, in which valleys, rivers,
roads and railways seem eager to guide the enemy.

Awkward as it is in relief, the north-east frontier
is not less awkward because of its salient outline. The
adversary who strikes simultaneously in Flanders, in
the Ardennes, in Lorraine, in Alsace and at the gates
of Burgundy, is delivering converging blows. If he
succeeds at one point, he shatters the whole system of
the French defence. The first forward steps take him
to the Seine, the Aube, the Marne, the Aisne and the
Oise, from which he has then only to follow the easiest
of paths to strike at her heart, Paris, which is at the
confluence of these rivers.

This breach in the ramparts is the age-old weakness
of the country. Through it, Roman Gaul saw the
Barbarians hurl themselves upon her wealth. It was
there that the Monarchy struggled to resist the pressure
of the Holy Roman Empire. There, Louis XIV
defended his power against the combined forces of
Europe. The Revolution all but came to grief there.
Napoleon succumbed there. In 1870, disaster and
shame advanced along the same road. In this fatal
passage-way we recently buried one-third of our
young men. Quite apart from war crises, with what
a heavy load has the possessions of this weak frontier
burdened France !

How many projects have proved abortive, how many

hopes have been shattered, how many enterprises brought to nothing, all for want of a good hedge around the estate ! The command of the sea has been lost, our expansion has been mortgaged, we have made alliances for which we pay too dearly, we have to submit to extortion and have been forced to abandon positions, and the people themselves, ceaselessly obsessed by the same threat, are in a constant state of uneasiness, division and irritation.

Besides, this chronic danger becomes greater as time goes on. For Paris to be where she is no doubt mattered little to a Carolingian. People living under the Capets took a more serious view of the situation. Under the Valois, they thought of little else. Under the Bourbons it became intolerable. Nineteenth-century France endured its crushing slavery. Think of it during the Great War ! What will it be like to-morrow ? There are but a hundred and twenty-five miles between Paris and the frontier, six days' march, three hours by motor-car, an hour by aeroplane. A single reverse at the sources of the Oise, and the Louvre is within gun range. And how is the rôle of Paris to be defined, unless, with Valéry, as prodigious and peculiar to itself ? This agglomeration, which is scarcely five miles across, controls the whole existence of the nation. Out of every seven Frenchmen, one lives there and the other six depend upon what people think there and what they do there. Doctrines, power, reputations, fashions, money, the fruits of the soil, the products of industry, flow into it and are redistributed by the currents of thought, of opinion and of transport, of which the capital is the focus. Its welfare or its downfall are very nearly commensurate with the health or ruin of the State itself. Each time Paris was taken during the last century, French resistance crumbled within an hour. Our national defence is essentially that of Paris.

Again, a large part of the necessities of our existence is found concentrated quite close to the worst part of our frontier. This was not always so. Provence, Aquitaine, the valleys of the Saone, and of the Rhone and the banks of the Loire successively held this position in former times. But at the present day, the world is machine-made. Of the coal produced by France, two-thirds comes out of the earth at Lens or at Valenciennes. Our rich iron ores come from Longwy, Briey, Nancy. The small amount of oil that we can extract gushes from the soil of Alsace. Of one-hundred-and-fifty blast furnaces, one-hundred-and-twenty are situated in Lorraine or in Champagne. North of the Seine valley, nine-tenths of French cloth and four-fifths of French woollen goods are woven. On the banks of that river the greater part of our chemical products, all our motor-cars, all our aircraft, are manufactured. In Brie, Beauce, Flanders, and Artois, are our best cornfields ; our sugar-beet is in Picardy and in Ile-de-France. The Paris basin provides a livelihood for fifteen million Frenchmen, those who produce the most and who own two-thirds of the country's wealth. Again, hardly has one crossed the Belgian frontier when one is in the centre of the industrial district of Roubaix, of the mines of Denain-Anzin or of the Meuse forges. It is but a day's march from Sierck to the Thionville blast furnaces. From Germany, Pechel-

French Heavy Tank in Action

"Not a few, but thousands of this latest type were needed"

French Medium Tanks in Action

"The results which a century ago many soldiers in concert achieved with difficulty are now speedily accomplished by a few perfected machines"

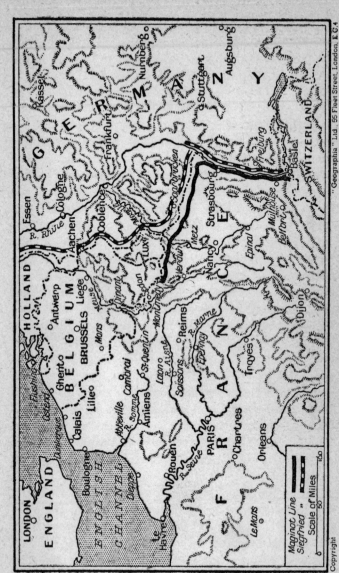

THE INVASION AREA

bronn is within gunfire and Strasbourg is within rifle-
fire. There are no steps leading up to our treasures.

Such geographical disadvantages are peculiar to
France. The sea protects England, America, and
Japan. The immense arc of the Alps prevents access
to Italy on all sides. Distance makes Russia impreg-
nable. The Pyrenees and, beyond them, great rugged
stretches of territory, defend Spain. How distant and
scattered are the active centres of the German Empire:
the Ruhr, the Harz Mountains, Saxony, Silesia ! To
reach them, we have first to cross the obstacle pre-
sented by a range of slaty mountains, narrow valleys,
precipitous slopes, and deep forests, forbidding and
misty, tortuous and treacherous. No one has ever
been able to cross the Rhine and invade German
territory. The land itself fights against the invader
with all its accidental features. If the invader takes
the Southern route, twenty mountain ranges, Bavarian,
Hessian, Westphalian, Suabian, Franconian, Thurin-
gian and Saxon, running in all directions, conspire to
confuse him. But if he marches in the North, the
numbers of rivers cutting across his route, of fens, of
bogs, sand-wastes and swamps, spread indefinitely
over the countryside, sadly wear out his strength and
his courage. That is the old story of Varus, of Soubise,
and of Moreau ; and the cause of Foch's supreme
hesitation.

In the five hours' flight by the Berlin-Paris air route,
the traveller sees, marked out on the soil, the safe-
guards of Germany and the weaknesses of France. On
leaving the banks of the Spree he can, during his long
enforced leisure over two-hundred-and-fifty miles as

far as the Meuse, pick out the moats in the shape of the Elbe, the Aller, the Leine, the Weser, and the Rhine, which protect the capital of the German State far and near ; he can contemplate the fortresses of the Harz, Hessian, Rothhaar, and Eifel mountains with which nature has endowed the Germans. Suddenly the land flattens out, grows gentler and more human. There are no longer any mountains or gorges or precipices. We have arrived in France ! Hardly is the frontier crossed than this basin-shaped territory which dips towards its centre, those converging rivers, railways and roads, this suburban aspect which the country assumes so rapidly, make one feel that Paris is quite close. And here at once we see the public buildings, warehouses and factories, the focus of a thousand arteries, ill-guarded by low hills, bordered by easily penetrated woods, without any fortifications, a close, coveted and easy prey !

## II

The policy of a State, said Napoleon, is decided by its geography. France has, through the centuries, sought by diplomacy the protection which nature has denied her. Others have been able to concentrate on the domination of the seas, the exploitation of distant lands and of free outlets, the uniting of a scattered race ; but what haunts us most is the safety of our own hexagonal territory. All the schemes prepared and treaties concluded by France during the past thousand years have had as their object the establishment of a political system which should prevent our enemies from molesting us. Thanks to these constantly renewed efforts, we have, indeed, survived, but we are now more than ever bereft of guarantees.

It is true that the last invasion from England was more than a century ago. After so many encounters, London and Paris have settled their differences. In return for the acknowledgment of British maritime supremacy, we are allowed to count on English neutrality, which may turn that neutrality into an alliance for mutual interest. No doubt, our Spanish quarrels have faded into the distant past also. For two hundred years Madrid, cut off from the Germans, far away from the Netherlands, troubled by separatisms, first ruined by its empire, then decaying through having lost it, placed until yesterday under the Bourbon sceptre, has been careful not to draw the sword against us except in case of legitimate self-defence. No doubt, also, the friendship of the Swiss, fostered by all our administrations and especially precious to-day, bars the entry via Burgundy and the Rhone valley. No doubt, lastly, after having so often attempted to negotiate with Italy, we have at least been able to achieve our national unity in the South-East and to persuade Piedmont, until recently the door-keeper of the Alps, to deliver up the keys of our mountains. But in Italy herself a great State has arisen whose fever for expansion has driven her into nightmares of empire. Our wealth tempts this nation, which is encouraged in its covetousness by the threat with which the feeblest of our frontiers is menaced by the strongest of our neighbours.

For, between Gauls and Teutons alternate victories have solved nothing and fulfilled nothing. At times, exhausted by war, the two nations seem to be reconciled, in the way that tottering wrestlers lean against one another for support. But, as soon as they recover, each resumes his watch upon his adversary. Such instability is in the nature of things. There is no geographic obstacle to keep the two races apart. The perpetual osmosis that has resulted from this has certainly had the effect of multiplying reciprocal influences, but it also makes any limit to the field of action purely arbitrary. Wherever it passes, the Franco-German frontier is an open wound. From whatever point it blows, the wind which sweeps it is laden with ulterior motives.

Conflicting temperaments fan this bitterness. It is not as though each underrated the value of the other and did not dream from time to time of the great things they could do together. But their reactions are so different that they keep the two nations in a constant state of distrust of each other. This Frenchman, who has so much order in his mind and so little in his acts, this logician who doubts everything, this lackadaisical hard worker, this stay-at-home colonizer, this enthusiast about alexandrines, tail-coats and public gardens, who, nevertheless, sings comic songs, goes about in sloppy clothes and strews the grass with litter, this Colbert colleague of Louvois, this Jacobin shouting "Long live the Emperor!" this politician who forms the "Union Sacrée", this man defeated at Charleroi who attacks on the Marne, in short, this fickle, uncertain, contradictory nation, how could the Teuton sympathize with it, understand it, or trust it? And, conversely, we feel uneasy about Germany, a force of the nature to which she clings so closely, a bundle of powerful yet hazy instincts, born artists without any taste, technicians who remain feudal, bellicose fathers of families, with restaurants which are temples, factories in the midst of forests, gothic palaces for lavatories, oppressors who want to be loved, separatists who are slavishly obedient, carpet-knights who make themselves sick when they have had too much beer, a road which Siegfried the Limousin sees as epic in the morning, romantic towards midday, warlike in the evening, a sublime and livid ocean from which the net draws out a jumble of monsters and treasures, a cathedral whose many coloured nave —an assembly of noble arches filled with harmonious tones—organizes, in symphonic harmony for the senses, for the mind, for the soul, the emotion and light and religion of the world, but whose transept is dark and echoes with low mutterings.

For centuries our rulers succeeded in limiting the dangers of the East by a traditional policy which kept our neighbours apart. Whether France employed arms to roll back the frontier, pleading in turn the rights of inheritance, the law of the stronger, the protection of others or liberty, or whether she possessed in Lorraine, on the Rhine, or in Holland, a number of sympathizers or of people bound together by common interest, or whether she exploited the Teuton tendency towards the clan, towards separate grouping, towards particularism, or whether she concluded balancing alliances behind their backs, she was, until comparatively recent times, able to prevent Germany from ever bringing her whole weight to bear upon her. But this classic game of chess in which, by combining force with intrigue, we held the fury of the Teutons at bay, has been swept from the board. Gone are the Protestant Princes who braved Charles V, the Suleimans let loose on Vienna, Gustavus Adolphus to aid Richelieu, the venal Prince-Bishops, alliances to be upset, the Confederation of the Rhine, rivalries between Hapsburgs and Hohenzollerns, and secret ambitions of Wittelsbachs. United Germany, favoured by our illusions, cemented by our disasters, consolidated by our haste to limit the results of our recent victory of 1918, has put the colossus in a position to hurl itself upon the West in a single instantaneous bound. Not, indeed, without many internal vexations. It is irksome for a Bavarian to accept Prussian domination, for a Rhenish Catholic to live under the authority of Protestant officials, for a Hamburg merchant to submit to the same regime as a small Pomeranian squire. In spite of appearances, all these regions, parties, powers and associations seethe with a thousand divergent inclinations. But it is just this threat of anarchy that eggs on the German Empire to undertake great enterprises. Its continued unity depends upon outside expansion and great designs, which alone in the eyes of the Germans justify the sacrifices they make for them. Bismarck understood this at first; when he seemed to forget it, a young emperor turned him out, with the approval of everyone. To-day, the Reich follows along the same lines. Who can doubt that a fresh crisis will once more draw the Germans towards Paris?

By what road do we imagine that the main part of their army will try to make its way? It is a fact that two hostile masses usually go the shortest way about attacking one another. The line which joins their centre of gravity marks the direction of their principal efforts. In the time of the Germani, a pastoral and hunting people, most of the population lived in the Northern plains. When the Roman Empire became too feeble to hold the Rhine, invasion started through Cologne and by the coast. Following this flat country, there was no fear of an ambuscade of the Gauls, chariots could be driven along without exhausting the oxen on the upgrades, and the sluggish rivers were easily forded. It was on the Scheldt that the Franks assembled. Later the Germans, having become an agricultural people, grouped themselves on the chalky uplands and the clay-soil valleys of the middle lands—Suabian, Franconian, Hessian, and Saxon, which formed the heart of the Empire. The Diet sitting at Ratisbon, and the throne of the Hapsburgs raised at Vienna, gave their blessing to this state of affairs, and German eyes and weapons were directed towards Lorraine, Burgundy, Franche-Comté. When France wanted to crush Germany, or vice-versa, it was in Bavaria, Franconia, Baden, Saxony or else in Lorraine, Alsace, Champagne that they met most often. The decisive battles bore the names of Freiburg, Blenheim, Rossbach, Crefeld, Valmy, Wissemburg, Hohenlinden, Ulm, Jena, Leipzig, Gravelotte ; the Netherlands only became the principal theatre of operations if the Emperors wished to join hands with their English, Dutch, or Swiss allies. Then the battlefields became Saint-Quentin, Denain, Wattignies, Waterloo.

But, in the past fifty years, Germany has become an industrial, commercial and maritime nation. Westphalian coal, Harz Mountain ores, and the great ports on the river estuaries, have attracted the labouring masses to the plains of the North. To-day, only one German in three lives south of the line Breslau-Leipzig-Cassel-Cologne, and south of this there are but ten towns of more than 100,000 inhabitants out of thirty-eight in the whole empire. Berlin has raised itself to the rank of economic and intellectual, as well as political, capital. For the greater number of Germans, the road to France lies through Belgium in the form of the Berlin-Paris railway. The famous Schlieffen plan was based on new and dominating circumstances. What neutrality treaty could have diverted towards Nancy a nation the mass of which was straining towards Charleroi? The same destiny may be played out to-morrow. Carried along by the force of circumstances, their direction dictated to them by their railways, eight out of eleven of the principal of which arrive at the frontier North of Thionville, invited by the level roads of Westphalia and Flanders and by the numberless canals of the Ruhr and of the Netherlands, attracted towards Antwerp and Calais by the instinct of keeping an eye on England, determined to strike us to the heart by the shortest and easiest path, will not the Germans take as their main direction the sources of the Oise, the worst flaw in our frail defences? In other words, the protection of France on her most dangerous frontier depends upon Belgium. If a solid Ardennes and Luxembourg barrier be raised against Germany, we are assured of time and space in which to act. But if the Emperor Otho, Charles V, Prince Eugene, Coburg, Blucher and von Kluck, as masters of the Meuse bridges, are able to make their battlefield on Flemish or Walloon territory, we see ourselves condemned to long and exhausting campaigns.

Now, although this Belgian country, without depth and without redoubts, this people of two separate races and two rival languages, this new and suspicious State, has proved herself able to play an heroic part, how many reasons may some day prevent her from committing herself completely, alone, in the forefront of the battle? Without imagining that the intrigues of Ferrand, Count of Flanders, should ever be revived, without even supposing that invaded

Belgium might wish to apply the Leopold plan, leave the way clear and arm only Antwerp, it is not certain that she must in every case accept the risk without more reservations and calculations than Albert I did in her name. In any case, let us not wait for her to tire herself out in protecting us.

It is true that France, disappointed by the old political system, is seeking, in a new international order of things, the security she used to find in her traditional methods of procedure. The dream of France, is, pre-eminently, that of an organised world, where the strictness of the law, the moderateness of desires and the ubiquity of the police would guarantee peace for all and allow everyone to live his own life. Tired as we are of adventures, well provided for in land and factories, overloaded with colonies, our interests become confused with this hope. Our love of universal systems, which enabled us to bear, successively, Roman authority, the gospel of classic laws and revolutionary principles, and perhaps also a particular tendency to open the door to new methods, must be taken into account. A thousand practical or noble reasons make France to-day the Penelope of international work. From this comes the network of pacts protocols and general acts which she is trying to weave around the world. Hence, in relation to others, especially the more restless, comes this attempt to appease everyone which she calls 'the European spirit'. Hence, also, with most of our politicians, comes the wish to turn the people against pageantry and strong-arm methods.

Meanwhile, time passes and it does not seem as

though all these efforts have helped to make France more secure. No doubt, by taking advantage of the credit conferred on our idealism through victory, and of the personal tact of our statesmen, helped by a certain Anglo-Saxon piety, it has at times been able to give the statue an appearance of life. But, first and foremost, there is nothing legal nor efficacious to oppose to violence. In view of certain abstract assertions and promises, the continuance of vested interests and watchful ambitions become unreasonable.

This liberal understanding of which we are so prodigal is not reciprocated. The egotism of nations becomes more and more stubborn. Each nation retires within herself. The world resounds with cries of : "The harm that has been caused me, the injustice that has been done to me, the territory which should be returned to me !" And at the very time when we declare that war should be outlawed and affect to efface the power of the sword from History and even its commemorative medals, in other places force is acclaimed, the nostalgia of danger is proclaimed as good and necessary, armaments are insisted upon and men are formed into militia, armies, and storm-troops. Where, then, will the torrent stop ?

# III

Is this poorly-protected nation, then, at least on her guard ? Does she seem capable of getting the best out of her war machine at a moment's notice ? Can she strike in real earnest from the outset ? Twenty centuries answer, No !

France, in a hundred conflicts, has proved herself able to make tremendous efforts ; but they were at first badly organized, ill-assorted and out of proportion to the eventual results.

No doubt, the fusion of several powerful races in the most favourable circumstances has created a 'rare and precious harmony' in our people. A country of mild climate, where every region possesses its own particular characteristics, complementing those of its neighbours, where the basins drained by divergent rivers of different character communicate with each other by easy passes, a land of harmonious horizons, of plentiful products, and varied in contour, France has imprinted on the men who live there her own stamp, making a balanced whole out of their differences and welding their many-sidedness into unity. History herself lent her aid. The Roman conquest, by giving the peoples of Gaul the same language, the same laws and Christianity and by making them accept a single morality, and later the monarchy, which was a force for unity, increased the common bond which withstood so many efforts to break it up. So, throughout the ages, we see France reacting in times of trial with extreme vigour, reconstructing herself when she lay in pieces, rising again when she was considered dead, in short, putting up, against the worst misfortunes, an amazing resistance and energy ; and she is strengthened by the obscure feeling that she possesses these qualities.

But the easy exchange of thought and sentiment among articulate people where everything comes from the centre, is bound to have as a reaction the fact that common impressions are fickle. This is a feature of the nervous make-up common to crowds and one which Cæsar himself noticed : "Gallorum subit ac repentina consilia." Enthusiasm and weakness, equally precipitous, plenty of passion but little constancy in our schemes, is our case. When we are surprised by danger, we accept it enthusiastically, but without preparation. At any rate, we bring no cohesion to bear upon the question. Every Frenchman is too concerned for his own independence. Before committing himself, he considers the matter carefully, acts in unison with others only when he believes it to be expedient, and reserves his judgment with regard to the hierarchy. Among us, solidarity and discipline have a quality of hesitancy, reserve and instability which make common action uneven and awkward. Moreover, when these doctrinal people meet fresh trials, they bristle with principles. Their eyes being blindfolded, they strike at empty air, rush aimlessly hither and thither, and hurl themselves heroically against brick walls. Then, discomfited but compensated by their pride, they find themselves face to face with reality and tear aside its veils. Then they embrace it, dominate it, penetrate it, and extract from it all the fruits of victory.

We have, of course, seen some of our affairs successfully decided from the very outset. Otho had hardly set foot on French soil when he had to fly on the night of the battle of Bouvines. The Flanders and Franche-Comté campaigns, during the War of Devolution, were models of foresight. The rumbling echo of the thunder with which Napoleon overthrew his adversaries is still to be heard. However, of the great conflicts in which our destiny was at stake, how many started calamitously ! How many absurd defeats has that evil genius cost us which, at Crecy and Poitiers, made us, faced by the English archers and cannon, confide our cause to the naive weapons of Chivalry, which drew the Valois into the crazy Italian wars when we were already menaced by the lengthening shadow of Charles V, which flung the France of the 'Rights of Man' into the struggle against Europe at the worst moment of our military disorganization, which lulled Napoleon with the dream of Nationalities while Prussia was sharpening her sword, and which, before 1914, blinded the ruling political school with pacifist illusions ! It is, of course, very fine and very pleasant to discover, in our extremity, Le Grand Ferre, Joan of Arc or Duguesclin, to contrive so well after Saint-Quentin as to drive Philip II from Paris, to be victorious at Denain when everything seemed lost, to frighten the already triumphant Prussians at Valmy, to strike again after Sedan with the mere stump of a sword, to win as if by a miracle the battle of the Marne. Nevertheless, these escapes from the

brink of the abyss do not, on the whole, offset the large
number of initial errors which make History echo
with the agonizing cries of our chiefs : the grim orders
of the day of Joffre and Gallieni ; Gambetta's adjura-
tion : "Lift up your hearts !"; Danton's outcry :
"The country is in danger" ; the sad utterance of
Louis XIV : "There is no happiness in our age !";
Francis I's sorrow : "All is lost save honour !"; the
Maid's tears over "our piteous condition" ; the despair
of Philip VI in flight : "Open the door ! It is the
wretched king of France !"

## IV

Gaping wide open, exposing her defenceless body to blows, deprived of all respite and all refuge, where, then, can our country find her latent protection except in arms ? The sword is not only the last argument in her quarrels ; it is also the only thing that makes up for her weakness. Everything that is ill-adapted in her territory, absurd in her political system, infirm in her character has, in the last resort, nothing to offset it but the warlike arts, the skill of her troops, the sufferings of her soldiers. And that is peculiar to our own country. The power of the United States can grow out of all proportion to its military importance ; lost wars do not compromise the future of Russia ; Italy came into being in the course of numerous reverses ; but for us, our greatness or our downfall depends directly on the fortune of battles. By virtue of her physical and mental make-up, France must either be well-armed or not armed at all. This is a harsh law which is perpetually at loggerheads with our idealism and our independent character, which gives our national existence a curiously tortured aspect, which constrained Mazarin, who disdained soldiers, to create the Royal Army, led Saint-Just into strategy, Gambetta to the Ministry for War, Rochefort into political intrigue and reserved for Clémenceau, at the end of his career, the enthusiasm of the generals.

The same conditions that from age to age compel us, whether we like it or not, to be a military nation, impose a permanent character on the initial system of our defences. Since the nature of things ordains that, in order for us to fight, we cannot afford a moment's delay, that we cannot afford to retire even half a dozen miles, and that a single lost battle means Paris put to fire and sword, our defence must be instantaneous. Other countries, when they are threatened, can take time to close their doors, to sound the alarm, to make the bull of Uri and the cow of Unterwalden bellow, and to call up their first and second reserves ; we have no such leisure. Especially as the Teuton adversary, a methodical organizer, excels in delivering extremely violent onslaughts from the outset. Frederick the Great's tactics, the mass warfare originated by Moltke, the turning movement visualized by Schlieffen, are so many thunderbolts. Once war was declared, hardly was the ink dry on the proclamations, than France learned that Brunswick was debouching into Champagne, that MacMahon and Froissard were defeated, and that "from the Somme to the Vosges the situation was unchanged." Nowadays, Germany is ceaselessly marshalling the means at her disposal with a view to rapid invasion. A certain portion of our own troops must always be on the alert and capable of deploying its whole force at the first shock of attack.

Again, this vanguard, upon which all depends, cannot hope, in support of its effort, to find any of those accidents of which nature is so prodigal elsewhere : a Thermopylæ in which to ambuscade itself, mountains for guerilla warfare, inundations with which to drown the enemy, a parched summer, a rainy season, 'General

Winter'. We fight our decisive battles in clear weather and in wide plains crossed by roads in good state of repair. Our assailants, coming up under cover of the forests of the Rhine, of the Moselle and of the Ardennes, find an easily penetrable countryside through which to debouch, and it is a simple task for them to choose their place and time. The defenders, if they remain inactive, find themselves surprised, immobilized and outflanked ; and thus you have Villeroi defeated at Ramillies or Bazaine blocked in Metz. If, on the other hand, they take an active rôle and are mobile and enterprising, as the Duke of Luxembourg at Fleurus or Napoleon in 1814, they go where they wish to, shelter at a moment's notice, and take the initiative themselves. This is the only sensible attitude to adopt towards the German, who, unequalled in carrying out plans he has prepared, loses his grip as soon as he is attacked in a way he does not expect, and shows an awkwardness in adapting himself to unforeseen circumstances that explains Valmy, Jena, and the Marne. It is therefore by manœuvring that France is protected. Now this perpetual state of alert, rapid and secret movement and the immediate convergence of all efforts, demand highly trained troops. The Committee of Public Safety might well punish the generals of 1793, but to win at Wattignies they had to wait until the northern divisions had acquired some sort of cohesion. If one only looked at the map, one might expect everything from Amade's group operating on von Kluck's flank after Charleroi. In point of fact, what did they get out of these still unconsolidated units ?

It is true that at all times France has tried to obscure

c

the breaches in her frontiers by fortifications. She is still doing the same. In the main, the same evidence by turns inspired Vauban, Gouvion-Saint-Cyr, Séré de Rivières, Painlevé and Maginot. One cannot value too highly the aid to resistance which permanent works are able to furnish. But these fortifications, quite apart from the fact that they must be given adequate garrisons, are very limited in depth. Besides, they leave the whole of the northern region exposed. And how can one foresee the effects that would be produced on the defenders by modern methods of attack, aircraft, super-heavy tanks and poisonous gases ? Moreover, one must take into consideration the possibilities of surrender. For, of all the trials of war, the hardest, on the whole, is reserved for beleaguered troops. The impression of finding oneself surrounded by assailants, the horrible feeling of isolation, the fact of having to live with one's wounded, the continual drain on one's strength which cannot be renewed, very soon undermine the morale of troops. And when to such shocks, suffered at the beginning of a campaign, are added those of one's baptism of fire, one needs extraordinary cohesion to resist them. Hence, of course, the supreme glory with which popular instinct surrounds the valiant defenders of strongholds. But hence also, of course, the complete surrenders which are the constant fate of indifferent garrisons. If Bayard and his faithful troops at Mézières, Masséna's men at Genoa and Rapp's 'old sweats' at Danzig—all tried and chosen soldiers—rendered admirable service, can we blind ourselves to the fact that in other times the crowding together in fortresses of hastily formed units had, as its chief result, the effect of filling the enemy's camps with prisoners and the Courts of Enquiry with their leaders ? To build our defence solely on the resistance of fortifications manned by novices would be absurd.

How, then, are we to compensate for all that is usually unsound and awkward in the initial actions of the French, except by building up a special body of men firmly welded together ? The qualities of a specially picked force can offset the effect of those errors of foresight, those illusions about themselves and about others, sharing this moral and material confusion which so often marks our encounters with reality. Method, the habit of not being astonished at anything, indeed that sort of isolation which long custom makes a sort of second nature to picked troops, those are the antidotes to our internal poisons. Behind vigilant arms the unrealities of politics admit of fewer perils. In military honour, there is a breakwater which does not yield to confusions of opinion. Thanks to the self-sacrifice of faithful servants, the nation will be able to avail itself, perhaps, of the respite necessary for recuperation. So one can crown one's king, form a 'League of Public Welfare', enrol volunteers, organize national defence or change the 'XVII plan', without risking the cries of "Everyone for himself !" and "We are betrayed" of a bad start. So, bad conditions in the initial defence of a country bring in their wake perfectly definite consequences. Geographically suited for invasion, exposed to surprise attacks by the tendencies of our own national character as well as by those of our neighbours, we cannot confine ourselves to hasty defences and disconnected formations in order

to resist the initial shock. The moment has come
when, to our mass of reserves and of recruits (the
principal element of national defence, but one which
is slow to mobilize and clumsy to set going, and whose
gigantic effort can only be used in the last degree of
danger) we must add a manœuvring instrument which
is capable of acting without delay, that is to say, one
which is permanent in its force, coherent, broken to
battle. Without a professional army there can be no
French defence.

*"It is thus ! . . ."*—HEGEL (before the mountains).

## TECHNIQUE

# I

HELPFUL FRIEND AT ALL TIMES, AT PRESENT THE machine controls our destiny. Certainly, from the dawn of history it had relieved the toil of our fellow-men. Raising or dragging heavy loads, crushing grain, preparing raw materials, it played its part in the labourer's task ; and yet without setting him free. Its slow power could only be laboriously exploited. The lever, the pulley, the mill or the press all demanded straining muscles and the sweat of the brow to work them. The primitive motions of which it was the extension and the amplification, had still to be carried out. Throughout the ages, neither the part it played nor its form were modified.

But the last century radically changed the relations between human beings and their mechanized servants. By applying enormous motive power, by perfecting their organs, by accelerating their rhythm, we found means of saving ourselves a thousand physical efforts. Machines which clothe us, warm us, give us light, transport us, prepare our food, help us to build and to cultivate the ground and to reproduce our thoughts, our voices and our likeness, have transformed the conditions of life more profoundly in a hundred years than six thousand years were able to do. But at the same time, we have become dependent upon them. The product of all these wheels is the criterion in the distribution of tasks, of ambitions and of profits ! In this way, the machine governs the life of our contemporaries in all its departments. It imprints its haste and its thraldom on them, gathers them together or disperses them, whistles them up or sends them away. It imposes itself on science as a subject upon which to theorise or as an instrument for experimentation. Art itself, in the jerky modern music, sculpture and literature, reflects the tremor of pistons and connecting-rods. Our sport and our desires are all haunted by motors.

Not, indeed far from it, that this slavery paralyses the capacity for invention in our race. For, if the employment of machinery sweeps away automatism of movement, on the other hand it makes technique more complex and competition keener. The Taylorian system implies the existence of the inventor and the specialist. It is by no means true that the mass of products thrown at the people by industry drowns their taste for creation ; in fact, it seems to excite it. The fact that furniture is turned out to a fixed pattern does not perhaps deprive the individual of the originality he formerly possessed, but it gives rise, in the most modest home, to a sense of arrangement which our forefathers never experienced. The trades which give women quantities of commonplace woven material instead of the rare and magnificent silks of former days, induce in them a very modern desire to be smart and original in making the material up. At the present time, one can drive forty horses at sixty miles an hour with one hand, but traffic demands of everyone, including the police, triumphs of ingenuity.

While mechanization has directed the activity of mankind in this new channel, military methods have also received the same impress. But not without setbacks, for in affairs of war, experimentation is sporadic. However, from crisis to crisis, equipment ever more powerful has been incorporated into armies. The results which a century ago many soldiers in concert achieved with difficulty are now speedily accomplished by a few perfected machines. At the Pyramids, a battalion square fired two thousand bullets a minute. That is now the work of three machine-guns and their range is ten times longer. In order to put her about, the *Bucentaure* needed three hundred sailors to manipulate her sails ; the *Lorraine* does the same thing with one man at the tiller, and another at the auxiliary motor. A single aeroplane in an hour can pick out more of the enemy than all the cavalry of Murat was able to do in a whole day. And while twenty despatch-riders were not enough to lead Grouchy to Waterloo, nowadays the movements of armies and fleets are instantaneously directed by wireless.

But, in their turn, by making such full use of material equipment, soldiers are apt to fall under its domination. Neither their bravery nor their skill can any longer achieve anything except as functions of the equipment which they set in motion. It is no longer a matter of making the enemy feel the strength of one's arm, but of manipulating a tube, a box, or a flywheel. Formerly, troops were bodies of men linked one with another, organized so as to assure the best possible co-ordination of muscle and heart ; to-day, they are machines acting in conjunction, and crews formed to serve them. If it happens that the instruments around which action is gravitating should falter, immediately military power is thrown out of gear. Just as a factory is paralysed by the failure of its electric current, so a battery whose observation station is destroyed is silenced. And one sees the divisional commander, when his wires are cut, as helpless as a financier without a telephone.

By being riveted so closely to the uncertainties of material equipment, military technique, like life, has become more complex and dependent on circumstances. In former times, it was limited to setting in motion a few weapons, vessels and vehicles ; now it involves an immense number of objects. The lance and the sword, and later the cannon and the musket, were enough for many centuries to settle the fate of the world. Alexander's piercing sight, Hannibal's single eye, Napoleon's spy-glass revealed the essential features of the battlefield. By means of trumpets, of stentorian voices, of banners and standard-bearers, and, in the last resort, of the king's white plume itself, armies manœuvred in orderly fashion. Now the infantry needs fifteen different weapons, the artillery sixty-eight models, and the engineers sixteen categories of units. The balloon, the aeroplane, gas, tanks, have taken their place in this system. The least action cannot take place without range-finders, photographs, plans and compasses. There can be no satisfactory liaison without a network of wires, of light-beams and of wireless communication.

In proportion, as the precision of so many instruments increases, so their successful handling becomes more attended with risk. The machine-gun can, in a few seconds, cast a hail of bullets into a narrow area ;

its efficiency is therefore either terrible or negligible according to the way it has been aimed. From his aeroplane, the observer can see clearly the action in all its details ; but if he makes a mistake, what consequences will ensue ! A miraculous set of orders will make a submarine submerge, but a control turned at the wrong moment will send the vessel to the bottom. Finally, the interdependence of machines has now become so great that it is impossible usefully to employ any one except in conjunction with others. The old soldier loaded his weapon, aimed it, fired it at the order, and was not concerned with anything further. But to make the most of a machine-gun, it is not enough to set it up, load it and fire it. One must, in addition, take advantage of the terrain, make use of camouflage, march, lie in wait, overcome night conditions, measure distances, exchange code signals with one's neighbours, make use on occasion of field glasses, of compasses, of maps, carry a gas-mask, handle a shovel, a pick, a sickle, an axe and adapt oneself constantly to changing circumstances. The army, down to the most insignificant of its members, is subject to the law of progress, in virtue of which every accomplishment which increases the power of men at the same time increases their labour.

Will the world call a halt to this frantic evolution ? There is nothing to suggest it ; on the contrary. Doubtless, an evolution so rapid does not proceed without some friction and resistance ; all man's conservative instincts execrate it. Thousands of employers, of workers and of economists resent the unceasing progress of machinery. Many soldiers of all ranks regret the changes brought about in the machines to which they have become accustomed. International conferences, like parliaments, re-echo with speeches at large directed against developments in the engines of war. But what happens ? Nothing can withstand the spirit of the times. That fixity of conditions which our fathers knew, in virtue of which a bourgeois of 1830 used for shelter, for clothing, for vehicles, for lighting and heating, and for the post, objects quite similar to those used by his grandfather, can hardly be imagined by the present generation, for whom houses, clothes, vehicles, electric light, radiators, gramophones, are out of date from one day to the next.

The same thing is true of military matters. Already the power of weapons differs radically from that of the last war. The firing capacity of a company of French infantry has at least doubled since 1918. What sort of showing would the types of aircraft which won them the victory make to-day ? Can one compare the battleships of Jutland with the new *Dunkerque* ? Nothing less than a feeling of glory prevents us from laughing at the sight of the taxis of the Marne. The developments of wireless telegraphy are making all other means of communication obsolete.

Modern conditions of military action demand, therefore, constantly increasing technical skill from fighting men. The equipment, which the force of events has introduced into the ranks, demands the gift, the taste, the habit of serving it. This is a consequence of evolution, ineluctable in the same way as the disappearance of candles or the end of sundials. The era of picked soldiers and selected crews has arrived.

## II

The metamorphosis of armies through mechanization naturally comes into violent conflict with conceptions formerly imposed by very different conditions, and finds itself surrounded by rules, conceptions and ideas, and military institutions which are, in some part, contradictory to it. The notion of quantity, taken, willy-nilly, as the basis of the organization and of the art of war since the end of the eighteenth century, supported by passionate political theories, hallowed by being so often put to the test, still dominates opinion, and, in consequence, everything else. Without doubt, the *Ancien Régime*, reacting in everything against the confusion of the Middle Ages, was able to put force upon a more reasonable basis, and pursue with reduced material a carefully calculated policy. But it was necessary for Revolutionary France to raise masses of conscripts, since the doctrine she preached raised against her a coalition of the whole of Europe. And Napoleon, in order to dominate the Continent, was very careful not to decry conscription, which provided him with so many men so cheaply. When the Prussia of Bismarck and de Roon wanted to achieve hegemony, she had recourse to the same system. As a result, the majority of nations, terrified by these upheavals, organized themselves in such a way that all able-bodied citizens had to serve in peace-time and fight in war-time. In addition, this tax of time, and, in the last resort, of blood, accorded so well with the egalitarian tendencies of the old world that it took on the firm and strong character of democratic principles. "Shoulder the knapsack!" for all and sundry—there was something in this that appealed to the general passion for levelling.

Thus, the tension which followed the Treaty of Frankfurt led the Continental nations to conscript whole classes and to accumulate reserves. It was a costly conception, certainly, and an emergency conception, but it was, after all, quite suitable as soon as citizens consented to do military service during three years of their youth and when armament consisted of a single type of portable weapon and a single kind of gun. It was just at the time when the magazine rifle and buffer-recoil gun reduced the work of shooting to extreme simplicity. Instruction itself was also extremely simple, and followed the same course from year to year. Army units, rigid and homogeneous, seemed extremely well adapted to a struggle which it was thought would be decided by the momentum and shock of masses.

To tell the truth, this rage for numerical strength did not prevent quality from developing its power. It was by fusion with the remnants of the 'old corps' that the cohorts of the Revolution found their equilibrium after many costly illusions. The Grand Army, which from Ulm to Friedland routed all its opponents, was composed essentially of 'old sweats.' When subsequently flocks of recruits, selected at random and hastily trained, came in and swamped the veterans, this solidity disappeared and the best conceived manœuvres failed in execution. Long-term service, applied by France from 1818 to 1870, gave her the best soldiers she has ever had. The army of Africa, of the Crimea, of Italy, abounded in warlike qualities. Although incompetence at the top brought it to a deplorable end, the rank-and-file, the poor rank-and-file, was, up to the very end, prodigal in the measure of its valour. During those three absurd weeks of August 1870, it killed or wounded 58,000 Germans, while its own losses were only 49,000 men. When its leaders surrendered its arms, it was itself intact. Hardly had it emerged from the prisons of the enemy than it found enough loyalty to raise the barricades of the Commune and save the State. Even in the gloomy hecatombs to which the exclusive system of nations-in-arms led during the Great War, the superiority of good troops was abundantly clear. How else is one to explain the prolonged success of the German armies against so many different opponents ? For the 1,700,000 deaths which they counted in all, the Germans, better trained than anyone else, killed 3,200,000 enemies ; for the 750,000 prisoners which they lost, they took 1,900,000. The well-informed understand what differences exist even in the same army between different units. Witnesses of the final engagements have not forgotten those proud picked troops, broken to every test, who in every action led the 'main effort.'

Nevertheless, whatever weakening of the rigid principle of numerical strength so many lessons should have brought about, once the war was over, that

principle resumed its absolute away. Broadly justified
by victory, sweeping and simple in its brutality, offering, in addition, the advantage of having in the
long run overcome set habits, it alone presided
at the reforging of our military institutions. By
virtue of laws passed relating to the subject, the
French field forces were formed by the combination of vast quantities of material and mobilised
masses.

But, as time passes, the inconveniences of the system
begin to show themselves. Military duty seems to the
French masses more burdensome than ever. What was
cheerfully accepted a short time ago, under the threat
of imminent danger, becomes irksome when victory
was obtained. Without taking into account that, as a
reaction against the recent abuse of arms, whatever
has to do with battles arouses the opposition of the
multitude. And then, life flows rapidly along, and the
time that is snatched from it to be spent in barracks
seems for the most part cruelly unproductive. As
always, these elementary tendencies assume the shape
of doctrines which are the meat and drink of those who
vie with each other for public favour. On the pretext
that in our age it is the whole nation which fights,
some are anxious to deny that strictly military formations have any value. By the mere fact of its rising,
the people will possess power, address and courage.
And therefore, to assemble permanent bodies of troops,
to distract citizens from their work and their surround-
ings, to inculcate into them anything, whatever it may
be, which is different from the ordinary process of
life, would be useless, even dangerous. Soon,

someone will set up as a principle that the less military training a nation has had, the better it fights, as Emile acquired learning through not having studied.

And so a blind impulse impels our legislators to reduce more and more the duration of active service. In the course of a decade, it has been cut down from three years to a single year. There is already talk of eight months, as a step towards six months or four. But who will believe that recruits passing by double shift each year into the regiments, even if they contrive by miracles of zeal to be taught the use of their weapons, will be made into war technicians? In the twenty-four weeks, to which in fact the instruction of each soldier is reduced, when allowance is made for the time wasted in calling-up and release, holidays, leaves, sickness, sanitary measures, fatigues, supply, maintenance services, it is asked of the infantry to train machine-gunners, riflemen, bombers, light-infantry-men, auxiliary engineers, pioneers, observers, signallers, drivers, telephonists, wireless operators, to make them as far as possible interchangeable, and to accustom them to concerted action, when it requires as much trouble to form, out of selected individuals, a mere football team. Groups, always provisional, which, once dispersed, are reunited with difficulty, like a pack of cards continuously shuffled and mixed up—this, in truth, is how our bodies of troops are constituted. Instead of the extreme finish which a methodised combination of activities could extract from a perfected machine, there are only hasty sketches. And since, on the other hand, the trained body of ex-service

D

non-commissioned officers succeeds in keeping out of
the ranks of the reserves, our mobilized units cannot
acquire the collective skill demanded by material
equipment except after long and increasing waste
of time.

One has only to see, piled up in the stores, the mass
of arms, tools, appliances, vehicles, munitions and
gadgets, intended for any one training-unit, and to
measure against it in the mind the flock of men without
experience or cohesion, who from one day to the next
would have to make use of them, to estimate what
wastage of men and of material the sudden test of
fire would bring about.

This latent opposition between mechanization and
the exclusive system of numerical strength cannot
fail to interfere with the conception of the correct
employment of various arms. Military art finds itself
placed in an equivocal position. The doctrines of
war are following, in fact—as is natural—the same
current which has taken possession of the age and impregnated it with mechanization. To renew the ancient
processes of manœuvre, thanks to all that modern
engines possess in the way of power, of precision and
of speed, is the task of the tacticians of our day. From
the point of view of art, there is there a field of research
great in itself, and one which could have far-reaching
results. In it, also, the mind would have the satisfaction of impressing on military action the industrial
and scientific stamp which is characteristic of the
present day. Meanwhile, so much effort rests on the
postulate that one can obtain adequate results from
personnel. It is true that this is a touching faith,

because of the willingness that it shows to neglect part of the real for the sake of what one desires, and to desire the ideal. But it is a dangerous faith, in that it impels one, in the sphere of the art of war, to erect theoretical structures which lack foundations. And so one frequently sees those in command indulging in tactical exercises which are unsuited to the instrument which will have to put them into practice, while, for their part, the rank-and-file make efforts which are useless, owing to lack of time to acquire the technical skill and the firmness of purpose necessary to manœuvre in the way that is expected of them. It is like a rash horseman claiming to get all the fine points of horsemanship out of a decrepit old screw.

Among all the reasons which go to explain the undercurrent of uneasiness which flows through the army to-day, this discord between the task to be fulfilled and the military system in force is certainly the chief. From top to bottom of the ladder, everyone lives under the impression that he has to solve a baffling problem. The high command would, at the beginning of a conflict, have to handle armies slow in formation, when the geographical, political, economic and moral conditions peculiar to France deprive it of any margin or any allowance for delay and impose on it a strategy of movement and speed. The instructors, who spin a sort of Penelope's web, handing on, from training-ground to training-ground, their elusive charges, are broken-hearted at seeing their men go when they have hardly got to know them. The reserve of officers are given, for lack of troops, theoretical instruction as to how to command them were they, by some chance, ever to have any under them. The soldiers themselves, who never get out of the phase of apprenticeship, who are jostled about among twenty different tasks, and bewildered by so many instruments whose effectiveness is ruined by their awkwardness, find during their military service or their periodical calling-up just time enough to learn in what consists that which, in order to do it well, they ought to know perfectly. The army, groaning, envelops itself in pretence. With what can the taste for what is precise, finished and carefully worked out, which animates our specialized and sporting generation, nourish itself, in a body condemned to perpetual approximations ?

One cannot be unaware of the fact that such lack of equilibrium compromises the prestige of the science of arms in public opinion. Force, in order to maintain its place, must possess a certain character of self-assurance. Standing firmly on his feet the Colossus is imposing, but if he totters he is merely pathetic. An intelligent public sees all the weakness of its troops spread out before its eyes : effective strength often derisory, because it has to be distributed over a large number of units and nuclei of war formations ; the perpetual dispersal of men and material and, as a fatal consequence, dreary uniforms, cheerless buildings, mean and wretched turn-outs. The mass of people feel that there is something inadequate in the ranks. In the dreary atmosphere surrounding its efforts, the army loses some of its glamour.

It is true that though the principal numerical

strength still stands in the way of basic reforms, on the other hand, specialization is succeeding in gradually penetrating into the stronghold to some extent. Behind the décor of institutions, necessity is doing its work. We see that the principle of quality, as opposed to that of quantity, is nowadays gaining ground in many branches of the forces. Of every two members of the crew of a French warship, one at least has adopted the navy as his career. And the other is doing his service in the navy because of his profession in civil life. The Air Force, except in certain purely manual capacities, consists entirely of men who have dedicated their lives to it. Our overseas troops are exclusively composed of long-service men. It is good to hear in Geneva as in Paris, the Ministers of Marine, Air and the Colonies reject as absurd for their departments the mere idea of short-term service. The whole police forces of the State and of the great cities are permanently in their profession. Even the fire-brigade, formerly simple-minded militiamen, are now everywhere becoming bands of technicians. And if we still cling, for territorial defence, to the notion of contingents that have been discharged with the rough corners barely smoothed off them, and of a host of legions dragged from the soil at the moment of need, no one any longer dares to sing the praises of such a rabble without insisting on more solid cadres at the same time. Indeed, these last are increasing in numerical strength year by year. In twenty years their number has doubled. To-day, there are a quarter of a million professional French soldiers. The professional army has been formed on the sea and in the air. On land the elements already exist, scattered and dissolved among the crowd. And as a reagent precipitates matter by concentrating it, a new technecial progress will bring about the formation of a privileged body among the soldiers. Armour will reappear, carried by the engine.

# III

Ever since Vulcan taught men the art of forging iron, right up to recent times, armour has dominated the battlefield. To be protected, or at any rate to believe it, is a great comfort to the individual and, in consequence, a great source of power ; and a great binding force for the troops, for the 'testudo' was not formed without order and discipline. Hence, in olden days, any nation that was rich enough and industrious enough to clothe its warriors in good brass had every chance of victory. This alone may be able to explain the military superiority of the Assyrians and Persians, and later, of the Greeks and Romans. It is true that one sword is as good as another, but those men provided with a helmet, armour and a metal shield and marching in close ranks, had an easy task against the Barbarians who were poorly protected by wood and leather and who fought each man for himself. Later on, the knights, enclosed in their armour and well mounted on horses protected by iron, could not fail to impose their power and force on the masses. During the battle everything depended on them. The fate of the non-protected foot auxiliaries, of whom there were many, was decided by that of the nobles. These lords, moreover, strengthened by the thought that they could not be pierced through their armour, were prodigal of feats of prowess. Therefore, without underrating the courage of the valiant Companions, one is not very much surprised at the piles of victims

slain by the heroes of the 'Chanson de Roland'—
including the archbishop—one can understand the
bravery of Eudes de France at Montfaucon, and the
fierceness of Renaud of Boulogne at Bouvines.  Great
losses in knights were only suffered when some cataclysm
or stratagem overcame the superiority in strength of
the armoured warriors ; such as when they were
crushed beneath the rocks at Roncevaux, tortured by
fever and thirst at Mansourah and at Attine, or
drowned in the canal at Courtrai.

The appearance of firearms brought an end to
these privileges and the musket bullet which broke
Bayard's back at Romagnano was a bloody symbol of
a new era.  For a long time armour tried to hold
its own, calling to its aid the finest steel ; but too great
a weight was required—not that the warriors gave it
up willingly.  Armour became, for the most part,
confined to the gorget, but armour was worn until
1915 by part of the heavy cavalry.  The helmet,
which had, since the beginning of the sixteenth
century, been the prerogative of special regiments,
came into universal use again during the Great War,
though the army did not go so far as to revive the shield
on the French front, as was done in the trenches at
Sebastopol.  These precautions, chiefly useful for the
illusion of safety which they impart, have not altered
the fact that, for four centuries, cannon-balls, bullets
and shell-splinters have pierced, torn and shattered
humanity without humanity being able to protect
itself from them in the open field.  A terrible ordeal
which left no remedy to the instinct of self-preservation
save to remain quietly in a casemate or in a hole in

the ground, and which distorted courage by condemning active and brave men to death.

But then the power-engine made its appearance. In its comparatively small casing immense power could be concentrated, by means of which the heaviest objects could be rapidly moved from place to place. However, as long as the motive power was steam and the engine itself consisted of very large units and required rails for mobility, it could only be used to dominate certain strategic combinations of circumstances. On it depended concentrations of troops, rocades, and supply. But it had to halt at the outskirts of the battlefield. A little later it entered it, thanks to petrol, which reduced it in size and freed it from the railway line. Soon it dominated the whole of the lines of communication, where everything that is mobile in the way of supplies and reserves depended more or less entirely upon it. Then, growing bolder, it came nearer to the front, moving lorries, tractors and light cars wherever the roads enabled it to do so. Nevertheless, owing to its visibility, its noise and its vulnerability, it did not yet dare enter the combat and remained an instrument of supply.

And then suddenly it becomes armoured. Crawling along on its caterpillars, carrying light guns and machine-guns, it advances into the front line, climbs over mounds and ditches, and beats down trenches and barbed-wire entanglements. However faltering and awkward it may have appeared at first, the tank completely upset the science of tactics. Through the tank was reborn the art of surprise, to which it added the relentlessness of machinery. Through it the art of manœuvring was restored in detail, since it could deliver either a frontal or a flank attack under fire, move and fire at the same time, and advance in any direction. Through it, above all detachments of fighting men recovered the mobile protection which they appeared to have lost for ever.

And this is all the more true because the tanks which are already in service, or are shortly to be brought into service, have left far behind the primitive forms in which they first appeared. Modern tanks each hold from three to fifteen men, who cannot be reached behind their armour by anything less than direct hits by large or medium shells, and they career about the battlefield at a surprising speed, firing in all directions. Their crews are protected from gas in their hermetically sealed block-houses, they can conceal their movements behind smoke-screens and they are in touch by wireless with the rear, with other tanks in their neighbourhood and with aircraft ; they are indeed the aristocrats of war, freed from the fetters which shackle the infantry. Not that they avoid danger, but they do indeed avoid the defects of soldiers in the open exposed to shells and bullets. For this, as much as for its power, the tank becomes the chief element of manœuvre and therefore its personnel has to be very carefully selected. If Pyrrhus chose his elephant-keepers with such care and Darius the drivers of his scythe-wheeled chariots, if the whole social system of the Middle Ages conspired to make the horsemen the strongest and most skilful fighters, how much more important will it soon be for the land battleships to have crews specially recruited and trained to combined action ?

Thus evolution, insofar as one owes it to mechanization, gives back to quality, as opposed to quantity, the importance which it had at one time lost. It is an indisputable fact that from now onward, on the sea, on land and in the air, a carefully chosen personnel, getting the most out of extremely powerful and varied material, possesses tremendous superiority over more or less confused masses. "We shall see," according to Paul Valéry, "the development of undertakings by a few chosen men, acting in crews and producing, in a few moments or in an hour, the most shattering results in the most unexpected places." No doubt this advantage will be but temporary. When once the crowd allows itself to be organized, and to be instructed with all the precision which machinery exacts, in short, when it ceases to be a crowd, specialized elements will gradually lose their relative power. But, in the delay which drags out more and more in a wider and wider field of action, and as the complication and scope of methods of warfare increase, the professionals, in their ships, their aircraft and their tanks, are certain to prevail.

*"Let us not claim that we can change the nature of things."*

EPICTETUS.

## POLICY

*POLICY* ★

# I

ALL THINGS ARE INTERCONNECTED.  THE TECHNICAL
necessity which is driving the military system towards
a professional army is adjusting itself to other evolu-
tionary tendencies.  For there is, in human affairs, a
sort of vague harmony in virtue of which the most
different forms of activity bear a common imprint.
It seems as if the political paths which the various
nations tread must lead them, so far as war is concerned, to the same conceptions, exactly implied by
the material progress of the time.

It is that, actually, the exclusive system of the
nation-in-arms is only suitable to conflicts in which
the stake is unlimited.  In order to justify a call to
arms of all men capable of bearing them, the death
of millions, the loss of vast riches and the social and
moral confusion which are the characteristics of mass-
warfare, we must first of all have violent quarrels, the
clash of frenzied hatred and ambition, and threatened
bondage.  That, at any rate, was the state of mind of
the nations of Europe before 1914, convinced that
war would offer them the alternatives of death or
victory.  Has nothing changed?  No doubt, since
armed nations destroyed each other, as we know, the
façade of principles apparently remains intact, because
the mass of people are reluctant to relinquish ideas
once they have acquired them, and most specialists
cling to recognized ideas.  This does not prevent the
conditions from which 'total war' grew from gradually

disappearing and making way for others. There are good reasons for believing that a war starting to-morrow would only be remotely connected, at the beginning, with the premature attack of mobilized masses.

And, firstly, the phobia of destruction, by which the nations were for such a long time tainted, has lost its virulence. The endurance of terrible trials shows the nations their vitality and demonstrates to them that the worst vicissitudes are not sufficient to destroy that characteristic material, and that specific part of the past and of the future which are the essence of each one of them. Even those who had, in the past, lost their independence, find themselves as much alive as ever. Cato cried out in the Senate that Carthage must be destroyed. France in 1793 was in danger of being dismembered. In 1914, France fought to avoid annihilation. But who believes nowadays that war, whatever the result of it might be, could wipe out 'Old England', kill 'Eternal France', or even erase Italy from the map?

Actually, as time goes on, the nations become more and more consolidated. Democratic institutions, instruction, and above all, the continual racial and social mixing due to fresh activities and communications, give the nations a deeper consciousness of themselves. Certain material and moral subjections, which formerly made political over-lordship possible, have disappeared. It is true that some States still keep the remnants of other races in their possession, but only amid a thousand difficulties. These minorities find protecting bulwarks in the vote in money, in Trade Unions and in the Press and they are helped from

without by innumerable leagues, schools, mandates
and subscriptions. What real and lasting profit could
be gained at the present day by disproportionate
annexations when one has no longer either divine
right, vasselage, serfdom, Diets to corrupt, clerics to
terrify, or nobility to seduce, nothing indeed but
violence to bind the inhabitants to the Empire ? The
world has become crystallized after intense dis-
turbances. The fiercest of men trying to disrupt it
would only smash their teeth against it !

At any rate, is it possible to derive great material
benefits from victory, such as those of which
imperialists dream ? While from conference to conference the mirage of plans, agreements, conditions of
payment, reparations, debts, wages, annuities, forfeits
and net balances was being dissipated, it was realized
that international warfare leads to the destruction of
property for which no compensation was possible and
that to insist upon payment of indemnities equivalent
to the amount expended leads to disastrous upheavals.

On the whole, the ubiquity of wealth, the over-
lapping of interests and the infiltration of ideas has
created among the nations an interdependence which
compels them to limit their ambitions.

Does this mean that nations no longer desire expansion ? Far from it. But their ambitions, however
brutal they may be in form, are certainly limited. A
sort of concentration on the objective in view is produced in ambitious men. They claim the Anschluss,
the Saar, the Dalmatian coast or a piece of Tran-
sylvanian territory, but they reserve the right to make
further claims when these are obtained, at the same

E

time taking care not to make exaggerated demands. Under the spate of invective which covers these demands, one can detect how anxious they are to remain within the bounds of possibility and not to set the whole world by the ears. They also take great care, in quite good faith, not to lay claim to anything save in the name of justice and not to threaten anyone without invoking peace at the top of their voices.

This sort of precaution in the choice of political aims is bound to be reflected in the subsequent form which the conflict will take. Surrounded by disapproving neutrals, flanked by suspicious allies, it is doubtful whether the aggressors would want frankly to wage unrestricted warfare for the sake of seizing a province or a colony. But in future the logical method of procedure would be to seize the coveted prize as swiftly as possible, thus offering the adversary the alternatives either of resigning himself to the *fait accompli*, or of assuming the risk and odium of a war of extermination. In any case, it seems as though the ambitious nations were getting together. Perhaps, even, the act of violence will be committed without either of the contestants having declared a state of war, so as to give general hypocrisy a chance and to avoid juristic complications which tend to embarrass diplomatic relations.

Of course, this does not mean that clashes between armed nations will not take place in future. After the recent hecatombs it is difficult for one to imagine a war waged throughout by a few specialized troops. Because one side may have gained an initial advantage, it does not follow that the other must immediately capitulate. Were it to do so, the victor, encouraged by his easy success, would no doubt wish to follow up his advantage. Because Manchuria gave in too quickly, the enemy were tempted to invade Jehol, the loss of which, in its turn, left Pekin open. After an initial reverse, a nation worthy of the name would want to return to the charge, drawing on its potential resources for the additional strength it needed. Moreover, modern methods of warfare, whether in the hands of specialists or not, have a disastrous effect not only on the combatants but also on the civil population. Cruisers making thirty-five knots and submarines which can travel fifteen thousand miles from base to base, soon convulse the lives of the people and ruin import trade. Air raids, heavy shells from long-range guns, and poison gases kill thousands of ordinary people and destroy any amount of property. This results in elementary reactions among the masses. As people's passions rise, in proportion to the amount of suffering they have to bear, we must count upon the nations yielding once more to the desire to enter the lists. But, even while preparing themselves for the worst, the victors would first try to cut the Gordian knot by a single blow.

One sees, then, how the professional army, ready to march anywhere at any moment, capable, thanks to the internal combustion engine, of reaching the battlefield in a few hours, able to produce every effect of surprise or destruction that it can furnish from the material at its disposal, in short, constructed in all its component parts with a view to obtaining the most complete and the swiftest local results, is in accordance with modern political conditions. There is a grim relationship between the properties of speed, power and concentration which modern weapons confer upon a well-trained military élite, and the tendency of nations to limit the objects of dispute in order to be able to seize them as rapidly as possible and at the least possible cost.

And yet our own country does not contemplate any expansion, nor does she desire anything but to keep what she has got. Strangely enough, however, this conception of her destiny entails certain dangers. For it is a moot point whether some great national dream is not necessary to a nation to keep it active and united. The clash of ideas, of passions and of opposing interests, in which the existence of a State consists, is in danger of becoming intolerable in the long run unless the citizens harbour a common hope which lessens the breaches between them and binds them together in devotion to the common cause. The desire for the Rhine, inherited from the Gauls, helped a great deal in the formation and maintenance of French unity. The rage of our forefathers against the treaties of 1815 counterbalanced for forty years the public discord caused by so many riots and revolutions. The thought of the loss of Alsace hovered above the political and social struggles of the Third Republic. And if the mass of people in our country seem to-day to have lost the feeling of the general interest, this can largely be attributed to lack of foreign ambitions.

But even if we were henceforward to renounce all expansion, the force of events, the accumulated weight of history, would preclude us from isolation. Our future strategy can no more limit itself to the strict defence of our territory than our policy can be confined to watching over our frontiers. Whether we like it or not we form part of a certain established order of things, whose elements are inextricably interwoven. What happens, for instance, to Central and Eastern Europe, to Denmark, to Belgium, to the Saar or to Switzerland affects us substantially. Again, we have signed treaties, subscribed to pacts, given undertakings, and adopted an attitude which, once again, confirms this interdependence.

With how much blood and tears did we pay for the error of the Second Empire which allowed Sadowa to happen without putting an army on the Rhine ! Under threat of finding ourselves here, there and everywhere faced with *faits accomplis*, and of being one day alone, without allies or friends, surrounded by the scorn of the world and faced by adversaries strengthened by their successes, we must be ready to take action outside our own country, at any moment and in any eventuality. How can this be done in practice if, in order to undertake anything at all, we have to mobilize our reserves ? In the present state of the world the very trend of our destiny leads us to make use of an ever-ready instrument of intervention for purposes of active assistance. Then only shall we have the army of our policy.

It is true that we try to consolidate this duty of protection in a universal or at least a European system. To combine the permanent interest of France with a great human ideal would be a great, and at the same time, a very profitable achievement ! For the union of nations to guarantee the good of each one would result in the transposition of a specifically French objective into the international scheme. So we must unreservedly approve, from the point of view of our country alone, of all definite engagements, supported by our own representatives, which tend to organize mutual assistance.

But how can we realize this universal order, this reciprocal respect of rights and frontiers, this mutual aid of all in the defence of each, without the co-operation, if only static, of force ? Justice which does not bear a sword beside its scales soon falls into ridicule. Besides, France has always recommended the formation of an international police-force composed of contingents from various countries. And of what could this force be composed, except of professional soldiers ? One cannot imagine Governments calling up conscripts and reserves to go and separate Japan and China, to occupy the Chaco, or to eject the racist militias from Austria or the Saar. On the other hand, one can well imagine that these professional contingents, assembled and moved about according to preconceived plans, and possessing sufficient military temper to be willing to fight without concerning themselves about motives, would seize a disputed territory, erect a barrier between the contestants and see to it that order was re-established. In short, they would bring to the maintenance of order an element of physical force which would certainly be more efficacious than any number of appeals. So the professional soldier becomes the necessary guarantee of all great human hopes.

After all, even if one could conceive of France deliberately losing interest in other nations and retiring within her own frontiers, abandoning the world to the mercy of wildly ambitious men, and, from the height of her ramparts, looking on at the massacre of the innocents in the plains, even purely domestic reasons would compel her to gather some of her children into professional troops. Our national existence has become that of an empire, and, as time goes on, this character becomes accentuated. The thousand bonds between the Mother Country and her overseas possessions are constantly multiplying. Not only because the task of developing the colonies calls for more and more energy on the part of France, but also because the restrictions on international exchange, a dominating factor of the age, daily increase the importance of finding fresh markets in our economic life. But, while under our ægis wealth, instruction and liberty abound, we can see the growth there of ideas, passions and interests, the obvious aim of which is the end of our domination. Of course, if we are enabled to pursue our work to the point of progress at which rulers acquire wisdom and the masses become loyal, we shall see populations, which are restless at present, sincerely accept the union. But until that time, we must remain masters, at the risk of losing everything.

It stands to reason that a military system in which the purely French troops are merely bands of recruits, organically incapable of going to fight overseas, is quite inadequate for the tasks which may lie before us. Although the devotion of auxiliary troops is an almost intact treasure, it would be, henceforward, impolitic to make them the sole source of our authority. France would be imprudent to rely entirely on native troops to protect the empire in Algiers, which reverberates to all the rumblings of Islam, and in Indo-China, which reacts to every disturbance in Asia. From the day upon which a force shall be created of men of our own country, who are professional soldiers and, in consequence, men prepared to go on distant campaigns, quite unconnected with politics, and from the day upon which, from time to time, we can parade some of our well-trained troops in carefully selected regions, from that day we shall be sufficiently guarded against danger to render it immediately less probable.

# III

So, the tendencies of the world, the conditions of
an international organization of peace, at all events our
own duty of assisting the weak and maintaining order in
the Empire, all combine to compel us to create professional troops.  One might be astonished that France
has not already done so, did one not know how powerful are the prejudices against it.  Above all, it must
be recognized that the military laws applied since
Versailles to our principal adversary, assured us, until
quite recently, of such a greatly superior strength that
it seemed superfluous to modify our institutions.
Everyone was aware, of course, that this state of affairs
could only be temporary, and that Germany, created
by arms and eager to bear them again, would one day
demand an end to the restraints put upon her.  But
certain politicians hoped then to prevent the unbridled
rivalry of force, by making a new agreement.  Having
established equality at a very low level, definite
guarantees of security and control would have prevented any aggression.

This effort at limitation seems decidedly com-
promised.  Besides, in a system based on the principle
of short-time service, it is confronted technically with
almost unsurmountable obstacles.  With the exclusive
system of masses, real war strength actually consists
much less in the peace effectives, the stock and calibres

of guns and machine-guns, or the number of aircraft
that can be described as military, than in the number
of men capable of being incorporated, industrial
potential, permanent air strength and morale of the
people, elements which, in practice, cannot be reduced
to any common measure. And, indeed, apart from
assurances of swift and thorough assistance on the
part of our other neighbours, this system of so-
called equality would have merely meant German
superiority.

These disadvantages, it is true, are held to be trifling
by some people, who are persuaded that the principle
of short-term service, especially suited for the defensive,
has the definite virtue of favouring peace, while the
professional army leads governments to aggression
because it particularly excels in attack. If one takes
that to mean that the State which possesses a Reichswehr will always have the initiative against a neighbouring State which has only a militia, the assertion
is irrefutable. But to conclude positively that the
system of professional troops is, of itself, more sanguinary than that of mass levies would be simply
absurd. All lack of skill is merely relative. Does it
follow that because an army is unskilled therefore one
must refrain from sending it in to attack ? Did the
volunteers and the pressed men of the Revolution
hesitate to fling themselves upon their enemies ? No
rival troops have ever been known to attack each
other so furiously as the improvised forces of the North
and South during the American Civil War. Bismarck
and Moltke undertook three great wars with troops
composed of conscripts and reservists. And we know

with what enthusiasm the untried American Army attacked in the Argonne and in Champagne. And again, the same popular instincts which in time of peace induce politicians to hope for the best, urge them to insist upon taking the offensive when war has been declared and rouses their passions. It is on such occasions that Saint-Just says to Jourdan : "To the wind with prudence !" that Gambetta compels d'Aurelle to advance against his will, that Briand substitutes Nivelle for the temporizing Joffre. To tell the truth, the application of the principle of the armed nation, furnishing inexhaustible resources, leads to the squandering of them and, moreover, multiplies those kind of losses which are, in battle, the toll paid by inexperience. On the other hand, the professional army, limited in numbers and difficult to replace, compels economy. Louis XIV and Frederick paid in men less for all their wars together than fell in the French Revolution. Chanzy saw more men die in three months on the Loire than Condé saw in his whole career. The whole total of lives and property destroyed by our battles from Joan of Arc to Rocham-beau did not reach the melancholy total of what the Great War cost us.

So that if evolution, which gives professional armies a growing superiority, is to end in the more or less complete substitution of well-regulated engagements for the frenzied clashes of armed masses, it would be a priceless boon for the human race. War is, perhaps, in the general activity of men, an ineluctable element, just as much as birth and death ; it may be that it is the disturbance necessary to destruction and renewal, the ploughshare in the soil, the axe on the tree, the battering-ram against the wall, but it is none the less true that its horrors depend, very largely, on the dimensions one gives to it. On the whole, no form of battle is more sanguinary than that of nations-in-arms.

## IV

Be that as it may, the Empire is rushing headlong into armaments. In the way things are shaping, our advantage becomes the supreme law. Anything, therefore, that can increase the relative importance of quality is to the direct advantage of France. For, if in former days it was to our interest to inaugurate the clashes of great masses of men, nowadays it is along another path that we must direct hostilities. We were the first, it is true, to make numerical strength the foundation of our military institutions, at the end of the XVIIIth century, and we resisted the whole of Europe for twenty-five years by sheer weight of man-power. But at that time the population of France was as great as that of Austria, Prussia and England together, and the country was wealthier and more centralized than any other nation ; so she had the best of reasons for waging battle on the basis of numbers. Actually, we were fighting two to one at Jemmapes ; at Wattignies we swamped the Netherlands, the Rhine, Italy and the Vendée by a wave of fourteen armies ; and at Leipzig we faced the allied armies with effective soldiers equal in numbers to all of theirs together. Even though this superiority gradually disappeared in the course of the last century, we retained the memory of it. Hence the deep-rooted illusion on the part of our politicians that legions dug out of the earth, when necessary, can repair any errors and neglect. Hence the partiality of soldiers for prodigal tactics, which, in defiance of all reason, still inspired us in 1914. To-day, alas ! our country is the least populated of all the great powers. For every Frenchman between the ages of twenty and thirty there are two Germans, two Italians and five Russians. No doubt our relative position improves as the birth-rate of the others tends to come down to our own modest level. No doubt also, our North African and Colonial troops afford us valuable aid, provided that we take the proper steps to safeguard them by imperial communications, the good-will of this or that neighbour and an incontestible authority over our subjects. It is none the less certain that future French victories will no longer be those of big battalions.

This is all the more so because the yield of our industry, however important it may be, and however varied and well balanced, in no way assures us of numerical superiority of arms. We are rich in iron ores, we have excellent modern machinery, sufficient transport, good sea ports, and we have at our disposal quantities of skilled and hard-working labour and a valuable technical personnel, so that we are, certainly, capable of providing our armies with powerful war material. But we are poor in coal, we have no oil, copper or zinc and therefore, though well equipped for moderate production, we could never surpass the mass production of German heavy industry. As for metallurgy, Germany produces twice as much steel and four times as much metallurgic coke as we do normally. She makes seven times as much machinery. As regards the basic materials for the manufacture of propellants and high explosives, four times as much benzol, ten times as much cellulose and twelve times as much nitrate are produced by the great German enterprises as issue from our own factories. A production of synthetic organic colouring matters, at least treble that of ours, assures our rivals of a great advantage in the future supply of war gases. Moreover, we may presume that we shall leave the initiative in starting a war to the enemy. There is nothing to show us that we shall again have the support of the whole world which enabled us to get the upper hand at the end of the last struggle. Even if we were to throw into the battle as many units as are opposed to us, it is by no means certain that we shall be able, throughout the campaign, to put into the field gun for gun and weight of ammunition for weight of ammunition. In the competition of war industries we are not the best endowed.

Since we are unable to predominate either in numbers or in material, have we at any rate a natural aptitude for mass action which would make up for insufficiency of power? It does not seem as though the spirit of discipline, the taste for being herded together, the capacity for acting in waves, in which consist the massive strength of hordes, has been given to us to any large extent. Other people like following the leader, living in compact groups, doing just like everyone else. That is not our spirit. We do not like the strict order which is acceptable to large flocks. Our processions march in confusion, we dislike one-way streets, we are incapable of singing properly in chorus. Of course, we sometimes have to obey orders. It sometimes even happens that national passion or the flame of a great talent inspires us with an astonishing ferocity as regards our adversareis or ourselves. This is a marvellous reserve of strength which bids us hope even in the most unhappy circumstances but will never make regular provision for the future.   Moreover, the recent abuse of arms has developed in our people an anti-war psychosis which is being carried to excess. Doctrines, pictures and allegories lavishly spread about, try to exorcise the phantoms of war. Even the past, so profusely battle-scarred, is suspect.

And while this depression increases the gaps in our war cohesion, all around us ambitious nations are reinforcing their natural inclinations towards enlistment with a policy of public spirit. The education of children, the sporting training of youth, the formation of adults into groups, and above all a deliberately induced psychology of respect and obedience, inculcate into citizens everything that may make them likely to stand up to the test. Thus the masses, their national passions fanned to white heat, sheltered from speeches and pictures which might weaken their resolutions, permanently subjected to the system of rank, cheering their leaders and wearing uniforms, are ready to slip straight from peace into war, without any transition period.

Of course, we must not prophesy from these attitudes the way in which nations will react when the time comes. It is one thing to brave death from a distance and to assert one's rights at the top of one's voice, but it is quite another thing to make all the sacrifices of which man is capable in the full misery of war.

F

And as for our momentarily exaggerated pacificism, what will it amount to when the moment arrives? Probably little enough. We have been accumulating the vast capital of warlike capacity for centuries, and this cannot be very seriously broken into by a few years of neurasthenia. Under the disheartening surface a powerful stream still flows. Moreover, having seen the *Union Sacrée* in 1914 take the place of the bitterest quarrels of which the country has ever been the object, we know that the national instinct, when aroused by danger, soon sweeps away sophistry, as a wave dissipates the foam on the sea. But in battle it is not sufficient to rally in the face of the enemy. One has to drain to the bitter dregs all the surprises of the first clash of arms, the anguish of reverses, agonies of pain, the envy, rage and contempt aroused by the hideousness of crises. That is when the seeds of despair begin to be sown. It is expedient that France, while still doing what is necessary to train crowds to fight crowds, should have another string to her bow.

Actually, everything shows that she is predestined to shine in the realm of quality. Our country with her tinted sky, her varied contours, her fertile soil, our fields full of fine corn and vines and livestock, our industry of artistic objects, finished products and luxury articles, our gifts of initiative, adaptation and self-respect make us, above all others, a race created for brilliant deeds and picked bodies of specialists. Independence of tasks, co-operation of ingenuity, that competition of skill in the use of adaptable machines, which will, in the future, require fighting by professionals, are naturally suited to the aptitudes of our best brains. The same causes that give us so many experts in delicate work will also favour us in the series of technical exploits which to-morrow will give the victory to specialized troops. It would appear that Destiny, in opening out this fresh path, desires once more to serve the fortunes of France.

# HOW ?

"*It is by no means enough to possess qualities ; one must have system.*"

LA ROCHEFOUCAULD.

## COMPOSITION

I

A WEAPON FOR REPRESSIVE AND PREVENTIVE ACTION—
that is what we have to provide for ourselves. A weapon
which can exert from the very outset extreme strength,
and can hold the enemy in a state of chronic surprise.
The internal combustion engine gives the means of
satisfying these conditions of ruthlessness and of
suddenness, since it will take whatever is required, where
it is needed and with all speed ; provided, of course,
that it is well handled.

To-morrow the professional army will move entirely
on caterpillar wheels. Every element of troops and
services will make its way across mountains and
valleys on the appropriate vehicles. Not a man, not a
gun, not a shell, not a piece of bread, will be trans-
ported in any other way. A large formation, striking
camp at daybreak, will be a hundred miles away
by night. It will need no more than one hour to come
from a distance of ten miles, and across any kind of
country, and take up its battle position against the
enemy, or to disappear, in breaking off contact, out
of range of fire and field-glasses. But this speed would
be of little value if it could not be reinforced by such
power of fire and assault that the rhythm of battle
synchronized with that of movement. What would
be the use of moving from place to place so rapidly
behind the scenes of the battlefield, only to find oneself subsequently immobilized ? But modern technique
can solve that problem, thanks to the armoured car.

By pursuing this ever-widening path, the stabilization of fronts by picked troops, which warped the last war from the point of view of military art, and, as a consequence, in the subsequent accounts of losses and results, will be avoided.

Six divisions of the line completely motorized and 'caterpillared', and partly armoured, will constitute an army suitable for carrying through a campaign. It will be an organism whose front, depth and means of protection and supply will allow it to operate independently. Each one of the six larger units will, furthermore, be provided with all that it needs in the way of weapons and supply services to carry on the battle from beginning to end, even if it is encircled by others. One may picture as follows the composition of each division :

A heavily armoured brigade, moving across country as fast as a horse at the gallop, armed with 500 guns of medium calibre, 400 smaller pieces, and 600 machine-guns, crossing ditches three yards wide, climbing mounds thirty feet high, felling 40-year-old trees, knocking down walls twelve bricks wide, crushing all obstacles, barriers and hedgerows—this is what industry to-day can provide for every professional division. This brigade of two regiments, one of heavy tanks, the other of medium tanks, with a reconnaissance battalion of very fast light machines, provided with improved equipment for liaison, observation and field work, will constitute the principal echelon of the larger unit.

A brigade of infantry consisting of two regiments of infantry and one battalion of riflemen, armed with

40 auxiliary pieces, the same number of anti-tank
guns, 600 light and heavy machine-guns, provided
with special tools for quickly digging trenches and
shelters, equipped, as to clothes, painted sheets, trellises,
etc., in such a way as to offer to the sight, and thus to
attacks, only unrecognizable objects, will be devoted
to the task of occupying, mopping up and organizing
the territory which the terrible but temporary power
of the tanks will have virtually secured. The mobile,
but on the whole haphazard and short-range fire
which will be operated in concert by the tanks and the
infantry, must be covered, from as far away as possible,
by another much more accurate system of fire. This
is the task of the artillery, which will have at its disposal, in the division, all the various types of gun
necessary for the preparation of attacks, for direct
support, for distant or close protection, and for counter-
battery work. Two artillery regiments, one consisting
of heavy, short guns, the other of lighter long-range
pieces, will form another strong unit, completed by an
anti-aircraft group, and capable of discharging 100 tons
of projectiles in a quarter of an hour, to a depth of
six miles beyond the battle-front.

The division, consisting of three complementary
brigades, reinforced by a battalion of engineers to
deal with crossings and a battalion of communication
troops, will have at its disposal a reconnaissance
group for scouting purposes. This latter will be
composed of very fast whippet tanks, of troops brought
up in their train for fighting on foot, and of light
vehicles for distant liaison ; the whole designed to get
into touch with the enemy, to hold a front temporarily,

to cover a flank for the time being, to cover a retreat.

Aerial units intended, not for casual tasks at any-one's behest, but with a definite mission of keeping a single, definite general constantly informed and always supporting the same comrades in battle and lengthening the effective range of familiar artillery, will be the eyes of the main unit.

Nevertheless, in spite of the speed, the protection, the wide dispersal afforded to the fighting troops by motor-vehicles, armed and caterpillared, the mass and the conspicuousness of troops so constituted will remain considerable.

The size of the machines, their noise and their tracks will be such that, without precautions, the enemy will have ample warning of their approach. But it is of paramount importance that he should be taken by surprise. Therefore, methodical camouflage must be put into effect. This art, as old as war, and one which, since the last conflict, has been made use of in many desultory ways, must become an essential element of manœuvre, as important as gunfire or mobility. It is impossible to exaggerate the results which can be achieved in this respect by research and discipline. In particular, the choice of disguise for fighting men and equipment according to the colour of the countryside, the creation of false landscapes and the alteration of the colours of objects considered with regard to distance, position and light are only at their crudest beginning. What about silence, particularly that of motor-engines, which could be obtained, if it was at all desired, by the adequate construction of the machines? What, especially, about smoke-screens, clouds and fogs, whose size, thickness and placing can be adapted to circumstances as required? But to make oneself invisible and inaudible is not enough. There still remains the question of deceiving the enemy by means of false road indications, sham columns on the march, deceptive earthworks and lighting effects, artificial noises, misleading wireless messages. Each division will possess a camouflage battalion, specialising in these things, and provided with the necessary means of deceiving the enemy by simulating the presence of a large unit.

A light division will be attached to the ensemble formed by the six divisions of the line, for scouting purposes and to prevent surprise ; this will be of the same general type as the others, but provided with faster and consequently more lightly armoured machines, light artillery, and with more mobile infantry, since they will not be armed with the same number of infantry guns. Finally, there will be the general reserves consisting of a brigade of very heavy tanks capable of attacking permanent fortifications, a brigade of artillery of very heavy calibre, a regiment of engineers, a regiment of signallers, a camouflage regiment, a regiment of reconnaissance aircraft, a regiment of riflemen and the usual supply services. These will complete the army of shock-troops.

As compared with the total number of troops that France sent into action in the month of August 1914, this army will possess a firing capacity three times larger, nearly ten times its speed and an immeasurably greater degree of protection. When one adds that the whole will normally operate on one tenth of its front and that the professional soldiers get enormously increased results from their equipment, one can gather some idea of the power which the professional army of to-morrow will be able to wield.

## II

This terrible mechanized system of fire, of shock, of speed, and of camouflage, needs, for its operation, 100,000 men. That is, by the way, the effective strength of the Reichswehr. It is, significantly, the strength of the professional forces of the U.S.A. and of Metropolitan England. It is, finally—a noteworthy fact—the minimum of the permanent force which ever since Henri IV, the governments of France have believed must be maintained.

These men will be young. Military training, more strenuous and more varied than ever, demands a great suppleness of muscle and of mind. If the tasks which the professional army will have to accomplish require wisdom and forethought in the High Command —for one must be careful if one has only a limited capital—they imply, for those who have to carry them out, the qualities of youth—love of danger and lack of ties. These professional troops must have nothing to bind them : neither habits, interest, nor family ties.

On the other hand, professional soldiers must serve long enough to consolidate their technical and mental equipment, but not beyond the moment when skill becomes routine. For those enrolled for twenty years' service, six years will be enough to go through the course. After that, veterans while still in their full vigour, they will furnish the active cadre for reserves and recruits.

Certain people, it is true, doubt whether it will be possible to find in France, in our day, so great a number of professional soldiers, amounting perhaps, on an average, to 15,000 a year. It must be admitted that past experience gives some weight to this objection, if one thinks of the difficulties experienced before the Great War in recruiting professional N.C.O.s. In that easy age, when our citizens dreamed only of being independent landed proprietors or of retiring on a pension, the constraint, the poverty, and the up-rooting imposed on 'the wretched soldiery' haunted public opinion. It seemed at that time, truly, to be sheer bravado to enlist in the army, to drill voluntarily on the parade ground, to accept exile and hardship in advance. It was not, certainly, that the war machine had ceased to impress the masses by its atmosphere of grandeur which affects almost every-one, nor that, after so much misery, people did not recognize how necessary it was to be strong. But, even while shedding tears at the parades on July 14th, while singing Deroulède's *Soldiers' Songs*, while shouting "Vive Boulanger !" the people heaped sarcasm on the N.C.O.s and sometimes even blows. The most in-dulgent were ready to see in General Boum, Colonel Ramollot, Sergeant-Major Flick and Sapper Camem-bert, the ridiculous but real types of the dotards of all ranks. In fact, the military plant must have had tremendous vitality to have survived in so unfavourable an atmosphere.

On the other hand, this plant has a distinct chance of thriving among modern tendencies. What the military class has lost in the way of public appeal and official credit, it is rapidly regaining, and that tenfold, by indirect methods, or, as one says at billiards, "off the cushion." In fact, the conditions, and consequently the customs of life, are transferring to groups the duties, authority and favours which recently were the prerogatives of the individual, of his rights, and of his independence ; and soon the law itself will follow suit. A society which forms itself into unions, accepts plenary powers, works in shifts at fixed rates, to a stereotyped model, and wants one-price clothes, tariffs and schools, is no longer inconsistent with massed troops, strict discipline, confinement to barracks and uniforms. The competition, the haste and the crowding which mark our age, impose on all precisely that compulsion which is laid on the troops. Just as the soldier is constantly subjected to the restrictions of military regulations, so no one is to-day his own master. Furthermore, when one sees industry Taylorized, economy regulated and opinions regimented, one is inclined to think that the military type of organization is in process of becoming symbolic of the New Age. In any case, the profession has lost the strange and anachronistic aspect which isolated it and paralysed it among its contemporaries. Enthusiastic young men can now be attracted into the ranks, provided that the army is based upon those characteristics which dominate the present generation.

First of all, service in the professional army will offer full satisfaction to the taste for fine machinery. Leave to others machine-guns which jam, worn-out guns, ridiculous vehicles, telephones repaired a hundred times, questionable aeroplanes, crippled tanks !

That alone, one may be certain, will attract volunteers. In a community which is throwing itself wholeheartedly into machinery, specialists, whether military or civil, either work listlessly or put forth prodigies of skill, according to whether they have to tinker with indifferent tools or are employing the very latest form of equipment. The fact that our Navy has launched, during the past fifteen years, the finest types of ship, has had more effect on the quality of its personnel than any amount of posters could have done. The increase in confidence the Italian air force has drawn from the faultless performance of Balbo's seaplanes is incalculable. The professional army, a model factory with its thousands of machines of precision and speed, all beautifully geared and handled by experts, cannot fail to excite the interest of the young. It will give them, besides, that kind of prestige which choice machinery confers upon those who serve it.

Modern war, like economic life, unquestionably implies increasing specialization. The fact that the fighter must be trained to fulfil a particular function with great accuracy may seem to involve a certain monotony in his training. But that is only so in appearance, for in battle no one can do anything efficiently without working in with many others, with whose duties he has to be familiar. To-morrow, the good infantryman will be, no doubt, an accurate marksman—with several types of weapon—but he will also be observer, pioneer, signaller, wireless-operator, motor-car driver, gunner and camouflage expert. The training of professional soldiers will be as different in its variety from the drill of Frederick the Great or the

French Tanks

"With 5,000 planes and 6,000 tanks we have lost a battle; under the same conditions, with 20,000 planes and 20,000 tanks we will, to-morrow, defeat the enemy!"

Invading the Low Countries

"German Tanks, able to travel anywhere and anyhow, take a trip down the Sambre near Charleroi" (1940)

A picture from a German ..... ....

'schools' of the old system, as the life of the chauffeur, driving his powerful car along unfamiliar roads, differs from the dreary toil of the galley-slave.

Furthermore, the flame of the sporting spirit must be applied to the training of troops. We must put to good use the eager strength and skill exerted in so many fields of activity, the desire to excel which is so dear to the young, the fame with which public opinion endows champions ; in short, the immense expenditure of energy and enthusiasm allocated by our era to physical effort and competition. Essentially, nothing lends itself better to the taste for sport than a military career. There is no single military operation which does not call for skill, energy and self-control. There is no single warlike action which is not a collective test and does not demand the concerted action of well-trained teams. To obtain better and better results from tools, means of transport, of signalling, or of observation, to strive to become a crack marksman, an exceptional driver, a first-class camouflage expert, are the new impulses which will get the best out of professional soldiers.

No doubt, military methods will have to change as a result. The impersonal mass system of training, which is the only one suited to the elements furnished by compulsory service, is useless for volunteers. Instead of summary compulsion, competition must be introduced. Routine promotion will be replaced by periodical competitions whose results will establish reputations and regulate awards. For the easy-going and vague system of good behaviour in the ranks and of satisfactory work at the top, must be substituted a

G

system of competitions, challenges, and prize-lists. And so, thanks to sporting competitive pride, the most modern motive powers will be brought to bear upon military training.

Pascal summed up the condition of human beings in three words, 'inconstancy, boredom, anxiety,' and he prophesied the passion for travel which would seize them as soon as means of transport enabled them to move quickly from place to place. To leave home, to escape from one's familiar environment, to seek a new object in life beyond the horizon, that is what we want nowadays. Perhaps it is an illusion. Clearly, the profession of arms can supply this want as no other can. For crack troops are only trained in varying types of country. Professional soldiers would never be able to accommodate themselves to barrack-life, drill endlessly carried out on the same polygon, long route marches, never varied, life in fixed camps, in short all the narrow monotony in which from year to year the training of conscripts drags itself out. But being constantly on the move, taken from plain to mountain, from forest to sea, performing even minor exercises under unaccustomed conditions, kept on the alert by the unexpected nature of slopes or coverts, halting-places or routes, these professional travellers would at once have their passion for travel satisfied and be trained to adapt themselves to changing circumstances.

These master troops, well fed and clothed, carefree celibates, a source of envy on account of all the fly-wheels, cylinders and range-finders they will have at their disposal, ranging the country from April to

November and touring France while on manœuvres, will be easily recruited. It is impossible to exaggerate the degree of technical perfection to which volunteers can attain. It is true that France has many times in her history used professional armies, but these were, except for small sections, recruited by legal compulsion or formed of mercenaries. Their ardour was damped either by the dull 'misery of unwanted discipline'—the worst, according to Barrès—or by the latent desire to give nothing except in proportion to their meagre pay. At bottom, rage at having drawn the wrong number in the conscription draw, eagerness to return to their fields and their wives, or regret for their impulsiveness in volunteering, did not predispose them for acts of great devotion. Yet if the properties of arms could make of these men the heroes of Fontenoy, of Constantinople, of Sebastopol, what could not be made to-morrow of 100,000 picked lads, ranged behind the banners of their own free choice?

# III

None the less, the harmony between the spirit of our age and a military career will not in any way remove from the profession of arms all its necessary severity and hardship. The army of to-morrow will also have its 'holy wounds.' Its men will experience the rigours of servitude, the irksomeness of gregarious life, the stupidity of appearing to be strange creatures whom people turn aside to stare at. They will have no love, no home of their own. They will inevitably be exposed to bodily hardship, to fatigue, to privations and to bad weather. They will be the first to be killed in war, and in greatest numbers. It is well that it should be so. A soldier is formed by the trials he has to undergo. Valour is not given to troops like flavour to fruits except by going against nature. But the professional army will certainly give its soldiers one impulse of strength and compensation for their sacrifices, namely, the military spirit.

The military spirit, indeed, confers on the fighters gathered under its ægis the highest degree of power. Other passions or appetites may momentarily provoke the enthusiasm of crowds. But no power can be established except by the taste for living together, the desire for common action and the eagerness to efface oneself for the good of the community which is the life of this rugged spirit. This is all the more so since this spirit is not only the bond which welds battalions into compact units, but is also a pride of quality by means of which the worst misfortunes assume an ideal aspect. For this tyrant, which distorts each individual the better to fashion the whole, distributes rewards which are never lost. The grandeur of undaunted troops and the magnificence of tattered armies ennobles those it oppresses. In it consist the illusions of the conscript, the honour of the seasoned soldier, the tears shed on the last day of service ; and it smooths the path of duty. Companion of lone outpost, witness of dumb suffering, mourner at humble tombs, its soft rays gild the most obscure sacrifices.

Such is the power of this leaven of collective energy, that it remains eternal and universal The same binding power which welded the Roman legions together was to reappear among the English archers of Crecy, as also among the Prussian Grenadiers at Leuthen and the French troops at Verdun. The most different armies constitute, by their community of instinct and of tradition, the truest 'International.' In it there is a store of moral capital which no nation can reject without forgetting itself. And so, except in moments of madness when they are paving the way for their own downfall, nations, as a matter of principle, culti- vate the military spirit, as they do that of the family, of labour, and of thrift. Even when an upheaval of ideas or of institutions deflects them from it for a time, they return to it sooner or later. So one sees the Con- vention praising the qualities of soldiers for whom the Constituent Assembly had nothing but insults and threats ; the opponents of the Empire, when they become leaders of the Republic, forming sound regi- ments, when but lately they called for "an army which

was not an army" ; and the Soviets making every effort
to resurrect the Russian Army, after having corrupted
and destroyed it.

Clearly, the professional army offers the field most
suited to the military spirit. But something must still
be done for this conglomeration of aims and emotions
to make it a practical force in war. Human passions,
so long as they remain ill-defined, accomplish nothing
methodical, and so nothing effective. They have to
be crystallized in well-defined circumstances. That
is why there is always something local about patriotism,
every religion builds its temples, and the cult of arms
demands *esprit de corps*. And, indeed, all that the
individual soldier gives of himself to the military
system, and all that he derives from it in dreams,
cares and ambitions, are contained in quite small
military units. The army in general is an entity so
vast that its members can hardly visualize it as such.
But the regiment can be seen, can be measured, can
be understood. A man has his own place there. He
can be recognized there among others. Of a soldier,
the first thing one says is "he is in such and such a
regiment." Moreover, the emotional side of the
profession finds something to feed upon in this organic
grouping. The desire which is felt by the weak,
mediocre, transient individual to participate in the
power, the greatness, the permanence and the splendour
of a famous regiment is exciting and satisfying. In
addition, the aesthetic character of military affairs which
appeals most strongly to the senses, is most clearly
seen by the soldier in the regiment : impressive
spectacles in which he is allowed to take part, thrilling

symbols which he is privileged to see and to touch,
stirring bugle-calls, and music in which sings a soul
with which his own mingles.

Furthermore, tradition has always allocated to
each corps its own peculiar characteristics. But what
was found by experience to be a good thing in the old
armies, is demanded as an imperative necessity by
modern needs. The presence of good feeling in a
regiment becomes increasingly important from day
to day, from the military point of view. For, as the
danger and the desperation of fighters on the battlefield increase, moral cohesion becomes more and more
important. A chain of steel could keep the Gallic
hordes literally bound together. The whole duty of
Frederick's battalions lay in being perfectly drilled,
keeping their ranks, carrying out movements in concert
and firing at the word of command. The French
Revolution added collective enthusiasm to this. Then
came advancing by sections, deployment by bands of
skirmishers or by lines of guns, a procedure which
was carried on even during the last war. Up till then,
liaison, although of course it involved previous agreement of minds and wills, remained essentially on the
physical level between men who could see each other,
hear each other, touch each other. All that was needed
was gestures and calls. But to-morrow each group
will fight alone but will nevertheless do nothing without
the distant help of its comrades by means of impassive
messages, secret codes and impersonal time-tables.
The appeal of innumerable Chevaliers d'Assas to
Auvergne will be expressed by the conventional dots
and dashes of the Morse code. It is true that modern

equipment makes possible, technically speaking, this concentration of scattered units. But it does not prevent man from remaining the foundation of the whole : so that technical evolution demands more military solidarity than ever. In the midst of the centrifugal forces unloosed by battle, no unit will remain cohesive unless its bonds have been long forged by regimental life : mutual understanding, common habits, 'the honour of the ship'.

The professional army will be built up of bodies of troops. This will be not only in a manner of speaking, or as an administrative means of distributing individuals, but as the result of an inflexible system. It is a matter of military policy to proceed to organization, to the application of principles, to the systematization of employment in such a way that the corps acquire the strongest characteristics of permanence and originality. There must be no more transfers for reasons of 'personal convenience', no more de-baptized units, contingents drafted from one regiment to another, hussars turned into dragoons, riflemen changed into troops of the line. No more aiguillettes changed from green to red, altered pennants and regimental colours exchanged at the *Invalides*. Away with central and principal sections, distant detachments, unknown specialists, and men seconded for duty who never rejoin their units. Away with training carried out in a thousand centres, schools and platoons, teachers coming from outside, units made up of bits and pieces. Instead of the ranks being continually broken up, of the continuous stream of effectives and of the kaleidoscope of leaders and comrades, real regiments will be created. Constant in their composition, in their rites and symbols, renewed imperceptibly by the arrival or departure of new elements in very small numbers, always united in barracks as well as on campaign, they will lead that intimate life and assume those marked characteristics from which develops collective fellow-feeling.

Once *esprit de corps* has been created, it must be trained. The spirit of emulation will provide a means to do this. Sporting rivalry, as organized between soldiers, will only have to be transformed into regimental competition. Important meetings will take place periodically, this time not between individual champions but between whole corps. In a chosen stretch of country, in accordance with a previously worked-out plan, each in its turn and in the presence of all the others will have to bring into action its fighting organization in co-operation with the others. The number of bullets and shells that hit the targets, the degree of camouflage achieved, the quality of organization work, the number of objectives discovered by observation, the adequacy of signalling and the working of supply columns, will be the measure of success, the whole operation being controlled by a jury making use of cameras, chronometers and microphones. This comparison, made with the utmost care, will do more for the cohesion of units than all routine orders put together. By the award to the winners of banners, special places in reviews, parades, billeting and even in the grading of pay to the winners, the spirit of enthusiasm and cohesion will be fostered in each regiment. In addition, if regional recruiting is employed and local pride is joined to military emulation, the whole population can be roused to enthusiasm by these military competitions. When one sees what the meeting of two sporting teams means in our towns and villages, one can well see how best to make *esprit de corps* echo through the land.

While, however, the cohesion of the division must be cultivated chiefly within the regiment, the division itself must also have its own peculiar character in peace time. Ever since Guibert conceived the idea of dividing the army into great sections, interchangeable, provided with all that was needed to fight as an isolated unit, the logic of battle has never ceased to accentuate the prominence of the division. This is the inevitable effect of the development of weapons, which constantly reinforce the interdependence of the various arms, just as mechanization continually urges industry towards centralization. But as soon as it becomes evident that no one arm can do anything without the others, that no success can be attained unless it is consolidated by the infantry, that a foot-soldier cannot move a limb without the support of tanks and guns, that everyone is blind unless aeroplanes see things for him, that he is paralysed without signals and powerless if he is deprived of his auxiliary services, then the organism whose function it is to combine these diverse elements must first be very carefully trained. It is not enough that there should be somewhere a commander and a general staff, that their various tasks are mapped out and that from time to time one unit makes contact with another. The division must live its own life. Formed of trained troops, it will be able to practise the higher branches of military art. The various arms will be made to train together, not only by means of conversations over the map or in the field, but in fact, and in detail. Large formations united for several weeks each year, organized exactly as they would be on campaign, will cover each region in turn in their manœuvres.

Six divisions consisting of a specified number of bodies of troops, all complete and on a permanent basis, will be the backbone of the professional army. This army will be composed of 100,000 volunteers, young and specially selected, capable of moving at great speed by means of mechanical transport and possessing powerful modern weapons. This great body of men will be inspired by the military spirit. And we shall see how far military art and the strength which are the honour of the profession of arms can progress by the use of technique and in a system based on selection and quality.

*"Beyond doubt life is only a movement of matter."*
                                MAETERLINCK.

# EMPLOYMENT

# I

FACED WITH THE UNKNOWN FUTURE, THE HUMAN mind seeks a refuge, and usually believes it has found it in what has already happened. Just as the politician consults precedents or the jurist custom, so the soldier endeavours to extract from the deeds accomplished yesterday the rules which should guide him in the acts of to-morrow. If he himself has not had the fortune to fight, he puts his questions to history. If he has made war, he consults his memory. One sees the army of to-day constructing its doctrines, its plans and its systems in accordance with the vagaries of the last war.

This eagerness to rely on the past in order to picture the future certainly possesses some advantages. Apart from the fact that it is natural and instinctive it agrees with the conception, which finds so much justification in other fields, of the continuity of human affairs and their continual repetition. Moreover, all artists, and particularly those in the military sphere, derive much benefit in their training from studying the masters and masterpieces, for there is something contagious about magnificence. Yet this conformity must not become exclusive, nor this imitation servile. No one can be sure that a future conflict will resemble, even remotely, the ones which we have already seen.

Therefore, when one is considering the employment of a picked army, speedy, powerful and well-protected, it is necessary, as a matter of principle, and even though it demands a mental effort, to abandon the use of conceptions which were applied to mass efforts during the last war. In particular, the continuity of fronts, the delays necessary for making preparations, the impossibility of developing local successes, all of which are ideas which the force of events imposed as the basis of the tactics of numerical strength, can have no value. On the other hand, independent enterprises, surprise, taking advantage of conditions, are all in perfect accordance with the character of the new instrument. If one wants at all costs to discover analogies with the events of the past, one must seek them, not in the slow developments of the last war, but rather in the operations of the great cavalry of olden days.

Indeed, armies like those of 1914, slow in their marches and their deployments, reconnoitring only short distances, bound closely to their lines of communication, were unable to expose either their flanks or their rear. Strategically their columns and tactically their chains of rifles or lines of guns were designed to operate in one direction only. If they were threatened by defeat or reverse, they had no other resource than a precipitate retreat. Indeed, one saw it happen to both sides. As a result, each section was obliged to maintain solid contact with its neighbours. The rigidity of the whole, and, as a consequence, the maintenance of the line, became indispensable. To wage battle 'in combined strength' was the strict axiom. There would have been no rest for the opposing forces had not their wings rested on impassable obstacles—Switzerland and the sea.

"Rivers, canals, are no longer impassable obstacles to large mechanised corps"

Those That Fly By Night

Consolidation of the combatants in fortified positions did not change, but rather reinforced, the principle of the continuous front. If a local offensive succeeded in breaking through, all the efforts of the defenders were devoted to re-establishing themselves shoulder to shoulder. Hinging, bracing, welding, warping, strategic withdrawal, these were the master words of military art. Meanwhile the attacker, who by his very success had uncovered his defences, slowed down his speed the further he advanced, and spoke only of pivoting, shortening the line, widening breaches, encirclement, reciprocal support. Up to the last shot fired, the opponents formed two flexible, but never broken, lines. Foch's gesture of hammering with his fist on an imaginary enemy line, in order to make pockets in it, accurately reproduced the form taken by military action of the period.

The corps of the future will not be bound by these limitations. Possessing, thanks to its engines and caterpillars, extreme suppleness, able to come into the open as well as to disappear with great speed, freed from the necessity of obtaining its supplies from fixed points, in short, capable of moving its position, its direction, and its dispositions almost instantaneously, it will be able to conduct operations lasting some considerable time quite independently. And, from the very outset, it is during the phase when the belligerents are marshalling their material and preparing themselves for the first assault that the task of the professional army will begin. The initial advantage, which owing to its composition it will possess over all other formations, will make it possible

H

for it to gain important victories during the early days of a conflict.

As a matter of fact, the idea of seizing territory, so widespread during previous centuries, had lost its importance in the minds of French strategists before the last war. The fact that Louis XIV, for example, had suddenly occupied Flanders during the War of Devolution and Franche-Comté during the war with Holland, and had on the whole done well out of this ; that Frederick the Great had seized Silesia without any preamble, and had not left it during seven years of war ; that Napoleon had made it a rule to carry the war into the enemy's country without delay—these lessons seemed to the leading school of thought to be more or less out of date. Naturally, they wanted to take the offensive, and indeed only the offensive ; but only as a matter of principle, and without attaching much importance to the nationality of the region which would be its theatre. Everything depended on winning the battle, no matter where it took place. It seemed strictly logical to allow the Germans to reach Brussels, or to accept the necessity of withdrawing to the Lower Seine in order to hold a more strategic line. Perhaps this state of mind was the main reason for the coolness shown by the High Command during the periods of crisis. But, in the end, we paid dearly enough for it.

The amount of destruction caused by war, the repercussions on public opinion of invasion or conquest, the fact of being in possession of territory when one is negotiating, the rôle that certain regions can play in the struggle through their resources or their position,

have restored the utmost importance to the occupation
of territory. To lose Thionville and Briey would be
to surrender half our steel production. To accept
a temporary withdrawal from Strasbourg would mean
that we should have to raze it to the ground in order
to retake it. If the Germans cross the Meuse, the
battle is brought to the gates of Lille. If they capture
Antwerp and instal their aeroplanes and submarines
there, our communications with England become
seriously affected. How can we keep the passage
open between Marseilles and Africa if Corsica is
snatched from us ? And what communications could
we keep up with our allies of Central and Eastern
Europe if Tunisia were to slip out of our hands ? On
the other hand, if we were to get possession of the
Sarre valley, it would give us 10,000,000 tons of coal
a year. Were we to reach the Swabian Danube we
would be cutting Austria off from Germany. By
debouching on the Main, we would spur the Czechs
into action. By seizing Treves and the Eifel plateau
we would cover at the same time Lorraine, Belgium
and Luxemburg. Whoever holds Dusseldorf, paralyses
the Ruhr. If Lyons is threatened across Swiss territory,
its defence is at Geneva. Whoever controls Sardinia
is in the best position to dominate the Western
Mediterranean.

Furthermore, from an intrinsically military point of
view, preventive intervention may have a considerable
effect on the development of operations. In passing
from a state of peace to a state of war, mass armies go
through a period of crisis. However much care has
been taken in preparations for mobilization, however

methodically it may be carried through, it nevertheless involves general upheaval. All the time that the calling up of reservists, the distribution of immense quantities of equipment, and the numberless movements and manipulations which these operations involve are taking place, the slightest unrest is fraught with danger. The same is true of the transport needed for the concentration of troops. For whole weeks, trains, convoys and ships follow each other in succession in accordance with carefully worked-out time-tables, and in conditions of interdependence which make the system very vulnerable. One has only to think of the way in which the smallest details are mapped out, to realize the consequences that may result from some unforeseen hitch. In addition, units pour into crowded debarkation-zones for transport and for supplies which are concentrated there, and so make the period of mobilization even more precarious. Covering elements are there to do their duty, of course. But even they are incomplete and scattered, and cannot be strong enough everywhere to prevent concentrated and premeditated attacks. That is why the wise Moltke, who reckoned on the rapid advance of our veterans, decided that in that eventuality the German concentration should take place on the right bank of the Rhine. The fact that our best troops were rooted to the spot by the hesitation of the High Command and by a thousand absurd delays does not alter the fact that we might have fought the first battle at Mainz.

Finally, how is it possible to leave out of account the impression that can be made on units which are not in war formation by dangers which suddenly appear in the most terrifying and imminent form? The men who, in August 1914, found themselves subjected to a hail of bullets and the blast of big shells, suffered a kind of moral annihilation. All the resolution, illusions and bravery with which they had armed themselves crumpled up in a twinkling, leaving them terrified among the shrieking wounded and the rigid corpses of the dead. When, to-day, the historian tries to explain in cold blood the confusion of this first clash of arms, the calmness of some people, the disappearance of these and the panic of those, he must first try to imagine the state of stupor into which these confident people were plunged by this disruption. Later on, the fresh drafts did not have to face the horrors of battle in such a brutal manner. Mixed with well-seasoned comrades, and penetrating gradually into the area over which death hovered, they did not as a rule have to undergo the same shocks. But although people grew used to these things by degrees during four years of war, it must not be forgotten what an ordeal they were at the beginning. It has been found by experience that the revelation of fire inflicted on unsteady troops can have very serious consequences ; and everything demands that the shock troops, provided with the more powerful and surprising engines of war, should take advantage of them without losing a moment.

The action of picked troops, which are ready to strike at the very first hour, in co-operation with the Air Force, and, if necessary, the Fleet, and which are capable of operating alone on the front and to a depth of sixty miles, will adapt itself advantageously to the general and military conditions which will make possession and initiative the trump cards in future conflicts. They will be able to pass in a single bound from peace to war, capture valuable spoils, and spread confusion among the enemy during his mobilization period. Their objectives will, of course, be limited by the means which will have to achieve them. It will not be a question of destroying, by this initial attack, all the forces of the enemy, but one of getting in the first blow. In modern conflicts, where everything has its percussions and repercussions, it is well to show one's determination and to spread anguish beyond the frontier at the first opportunity. We ourselves already bear only too deeply the scars of invasion.

Being independent in its movements, the professional army will be all the more able to strike unexpectedly. Whether it is operating on its own account, or forming part of a larger formation, in a general conflict, the blows that it will deliver will be both sudden and violent. By this means, there will be reborn the surprise attack, which has always been the criterion of leaders, and which the last war banished from battle because every attack had to be carefully prepared. It was necessary, at that time, for any attack at all, that the ground should be carefully organized from the point of view of waves of attack and reserve positions, that all kinds of communications should be established, gun-emplacements built, stores brought up to strength, command posts chosen, signalling systems arranged and men and guns taken across the trench system. Moreover, what an enormous amount of time and trouble it took to get these foot soldiers into the line on a six-mile front with all their arms, ammunition, rations, tools and accessories, stumbling at every step over the broken ground, and under ceaseless fire. It was necessary, therefore, to spend several days in destroying the enemy positions by artillery fire, before launching assault-troops into the open against an entrenched enemy. During the final months, it is true, the fact that the offensive took place on the whole front, the lessons of past experience, the enormous quantity of artillery of all kinds accumulated in all sectors, and above all the appearance of tanks, which in large measure supplanted artillery preparation, made it possible to launch attacks before the enemy could put himself on his guard. All the same, to the very end of the drama, the unexpected was the exception. To-morrow, it will be the usual procedure of a picked band, organized and equipped to that end.

In fact, caterpillar-vehicles moving across any type of country will quickly transport to the point of action everything necessary for the attack, instead of it being brought in driblets by fatigue parties, on the backs of animals, by roads, tracks, saps and communication trenches. Six days were required to bring up the 10,000 tons of material needed for battle by a Division in 1917. The same task will be carried out in a single night by a Division of the new type. Furthermore, close contact with the enemy's position by troops about to attack will no longer be of any more importance when the storming echelon is composed of armoured vehicles. These, kept concealed out of range of the more intense fire, will only come up to the front line at the last moment, under cover of night or artificial fog. Finally, since they themselves will carry formidable artillery and will be designed to crush systematic defences, they will readily dispense with previous destruction of the enemy positions. The defence will have none of the indications, which formerly showed that an attack was imminent, and will remain in ignorance until the very hour when the armoured vehicles break into his lines. Surprise, the old queen of the art of war, which was consigned to the rubbish heap so long as power lacked speed, will find a new instrument, and in consequence will recover its power.

But surprise must be organized.  Not only by means
of secrecy, observed in conversation, orders and reports
by those who prepare plans and make decisions, and
by the concealment of preparations, but also under
cover of a thick veil of make-believe.  In our age,
when a thousand mischief-makers are mixed up in our
affairs, when honour is less persuasive than money,
when the Press is ever on the hunt for information,
when no enterprise can be carried on without telephones, wireless and typewriters, when all figures have
to be deciphered, it is almost impossible to prevent
information reaching the enemy.  But, none the less,
one may confuse him.  If one is willing to hoodwink
one's own camp deliberately, to mislead the very
people one intends to employ, or by clever artifice to
use all the means which are now available to each
side for discovering what the other is doing, in order
to spread misleading rumours, one can hide reality
behind falsehood.  That is how Themistocles used the
Persian spies to provoke the attack at Salamis.  Certainly it is a cruel ordeal for the man who has to do
the job to be kept in ignorance of his objective until
the last minute.  To bear it, he needs all the background of the military virtues.  Here is another reason
why massed nations would find it difficult to accustom
themselves to such a system.  But to picked troops,
trained to resignation, their leaders can promise rest
when they intend them to fight, can deny any
intention of offensive when it is already decided upon,
announce a march into Alsace when their goal is really
Flanders.

None the less, however great a faculty picked troops

may have for carrying out unanticipated orders, certain preparations will still have to be made. On the front, the enemy is on the alert. There, it will not be sufficient to disguise men and material. Cunning must be used in order to make him believe that one is where one is not, that one wants something quite different from what one does. In the areas chosen for action, active camouflage must be used ; specialist units will methodically lay false trails. The eyes of the enemy must be confused by the appearance of bridges, tracks, railways, by imitation terraces, batteries and observation points, by make-believe columns, convoys and troop concentrations. His ears must be deceived by the noise of moving vehicles, explosions, and the roar of engines. His mind must be distracted by wireless masts in action, by signals he can intercept, conversations he can overhear. Whole sectors must be hidden by smoke-screens, in order to present the appearance of false attacks. A sense of uncertainty which is very wearing for the High Command, the troops of the line, and the reserves, must invade the opposing camp.

Meanwhile, the shock troops, whose elements have been kept scattered until the last moment, will take up their positions in a single night, in order to launch the attack at dawn. Each Division establishes its base, while the infantry sets up its guns and machine-guns. In the rear, the artillery takes up its positions, organized, as a result of using guns firing at all angles, less for the purpose of firing profusely into narrow areas at particular objectives, than for intervention after the attack is launched. Its first duty is to lay down a barrage down round the tanks. This must be very wide and very elastic, as the tanks move quickly, and, on the other hand, the enemy guns capable of attacking them are disposed not in line but like pieces on a chess-board. In addition, the artillery must be prepared to concentrate a great volume of fire wherever it is needed, at any moment, so as to dominate rapidly any part of the battlefield which may be threatened. In other words, flexibility becomes the rule for a weapon which but recently proceeded chiefly in accordance with pre-arranged plans. The grouping of infantry and of artillery, the allotment of duties, the laying out of lines of fire and the battery positions, are all liable to continual change.

Some distance to the rear, the tanks are forming up for battle. They are normally arranged in three echelons. First come the light machines which will make the first contact with the enemy. Then comes the battle echelon, which is made up of medium and heavy tanks, and whose front and depth depend on the nature of the operation and the estimated resistance. Finally, the reserve echelon, designed for relief or for following up successes. Each echelon is itself made up of successive sections. On the average, the attacking force of the Division covers an area about five miles wide including intervals, the elements being more or less dense along the front according to the object of the operation. The whole consists of five or six waves of tanks, of which the strongest is generally the leading battle echelon. Even if the army only consists of four Divisions, 2,000 tanks, on a front of twenty miles, can go into action at the same time.

Suddenly, these monsters start off. The light tanks go rapidly forward to make contact with the enemy. Their duty is to determine the position and nature of the first resistance, to find out and to indicate the most favourable routes, to camouflage difficult passages by smoke-screens, in short, to reconnoitre for and to cover up the chief body of the tanks. Then when these tasks are carried through, the small tanks will leave the front, and take up their position on the flanks for observation or in the rear to maintain communication. At each lull, they resume their task of reconnaissance in the van.

But now the battle echelon takes up the fight in its turn. The large groups which constitute it move across the ground, not in line, but in independent sections manœuvring as circumstances dictate. Their line of advance is, for the most part, at a definite angle to the enemy front, in order to meet resistance obliquely, and to be free to change their direction many times in the course of the battle. These flexible units machine-gun the surface of the ground, reserving their gun-fire for special objectives which they try to wipe out by taking them in the rear. Each manœuvre consists essentially of turns made by the attacker in order to attack from behind, while the artillery covers the operation by means of fire distributed all round the area where the action is taking place and by sending out smoke-screens to conceal those tanks which have to stay in one place.

At the same time, measures must be taken to ensure that progress is not unduly hindered by slow mopping-up. The leading elements must therefore be used to break through and to push on towards the final objective as promptly as possible. Their supporting units will finish off what they have begun. If they are not enough for this purpose, their reserves will do what is necessary. In the last resort, the infantry will help in this. In short, if the enemy puts up a determined resistance, the attacker will soon appear in the form of groups of tanks figuring in great depth, while the first wave will have continued its advance and the artillery will have taken within its field of fire not only the outer edge of this whole field of combat, but also certain blocks of territory in the back areas which have already been passed by.

In proportion as the tanks produce their effect, so the infantry advances. Sometimes this is done on caterpillar-vehicles. Sometimes they make their way on foot. In any case, their task is to take possession of captured ground. This task is carried out by occupying successive positions, protected in depth with machines and machine-guns, rapidly brought into action. Frequently, they will have to reduce remnants of resistance by means of appropriate manœuvres and by the fire of their auxiliary guns. Sometimes, their lines will serve as support and as relief, especially if the enemy, having got wind of the surprise, has also been able to bring up armoured units at the proper time and place, and to launch counter-attacks. It is obvious that the occupation will be made not on continuous lines, but by strong detachments grouped round the infantry's machines, disposed at intervals and at some distance from each other, but in such a way that they are ready to give mutual support.

All these actions, naturally, are carried out under a camouflage of artificial fogs.

Together with the foot-soldiers, the artillery advances. Thanks to caterpillar wheels, they can push their advance as far as they wish. For them, there is an end of taking up position *en masse*, which, during the last war, was rendered necessary by the difficulty of covering shell-torn ground, the inflexibility of organization, and the slowness of supplies. If it is left alone, a group of artillery can leave its emplacements and take up positions five miles further on a few minutes later. On the other hand, the speeding up of battle will not allow the artillery to proceed in the old way, to share out their tasks once for all at the beginning of an undertaking, to divide the enemy territory into limited fields of action, to work out their fire mathematically, as they were able to do in the days of stabilized fronts. On the contrary, as soon as the enemy position has been attacked, they will have to direct their fire in accordance with rapidly developing events. In other words, the artillery must keep in close touch with the battle-echelon, not only by observation and liaison parties, but also in complete units, with weapons, if not with baggage. The artillery also becomes a mass movement, whose individual sections take up the positions best suited for action, and who fire from all angles at objectives which are almost continuously on the move. Provided, in addition, with anti-tank weapons, and machine-guns, the artillery protects itself by its own means. Instead of immobility, map-firing, and centralization, it must now learn direct observation and initiative.

A battle of this sort immensely increases the importance of the rôle of aircraft.   Motorized units must
have speedy information and be protected as widely
as possible.  The most adequate support is, therefore,
that which comes from the air.  For troops who proceed by surprise and speed, aeroplanes will be, in
everything, not only auxiliaries but indispensable
comrades in arms.   In order that, at a moment's
notice, tanks may be in a position to manœuvre where
they are needed, guns may concentrate their first on
the necessary points, and reserves may be moved up to
the right spot, nothing is so useful as the aeroplane
which discovers the enemy far off, rapidly signals the
position of objectives, and equally rapidly indicates
the position of friendly troops.  We are at the point
where the aeroplane will be the High Command's real
means of making, from time to time, personal reconnaissance of the situation, and light machines, capable
of landing anywhere, will have to be attached to the
General Staff.  In addition, ground troops, especially
armoured units, will receive valuable aid from aircraft
with  regard  to  their  camouflage.   Smoke-screens
spread from the air can hide in a few minutes vast
areas of ground, while the noise of flying machines
will cover that of caterpillar vehicles.  But especially
by striking of its own accord on visible targets, the
Air  Force  becomes, *par excellence*, the  arm  whose
lightning effects combine best with the principles of
strategic withdrawal and the exploitation of large
mechanized formations.

Inversely, co-operation with the assault troops will
demand from the squadrons brief and concentrated

operations, which are best adapted to the nature of
the Air arm. When the aircraft have to link their
efforts with those of men whose rate of progress is a
crawl, and have to operate day after day relieving
each other in the same sector, the risks multiply as
time passes and terribly complicate their task ; the
enemy's reactions in pursuing them, and in bringing
up special artillery, the changes in the atmosphere,
the damage to machines and the fatigue of the personnel increase. By contrast, if they can assemble
suddenly, and operate in great number for a short
space of time, their results will be tenfold. On the
other hand, their protection becomes correspondingly
easier, for, although it is impossible to retain permanent mastery of the air in a sector where the enemy
has time to take counter-measures, it is, however,
possible to seize it unexpectedly at one point, at a
chosen instant. The tactics of the new army, operating
by short and unexpected attacks, will respond very
well to the prerogatives and the services of its air
fighters.

Thus the battle develops, a tangle of actions con-
ducted with great speed, each one of which demands
the participation of elements divided into many small
sections. It is clear that, in spite of the qualities of the
personnel, this flexibility cannot be realized without a
rapid and accurate system of signalling. If one had to
stick to the old procedure, that is to say to the instal-
lation of wires, the erection of telegraph posts and
transmitters, agreed codes and signals, and chains of
breathless orderlies, then the same difficulties which
attend the laying out of the telephone, the exchange of

Morse messages and the dispatch of orderlies, would result in the same slowing-down in the tempo of battle. But progress, at the same time as it has introduced speed into the employment of engines of war, provides the means of linking them together in the necessary way. Radio-telegraphy has reached the point where people will be able to converse upon an unlimited number of sets simultaneously without interfering with each other. The selectivity of certain sets makes them accessible only to waves of a precise length, and allows those who wish to communicate to get into touch with each other without searching, and to isolate themselves from other transmissions. In addition, there are means of providing that there shall be no intrusion or interference on the specific wavelength of a certain set. To-morrow, the majority of communications will be by the spoken word. At any distance, at any moment, from a tank, a car, an aeroplane, the corner of a wall, the foot of a tree, the voice of the leader will make known to his subordinates, to his equals, to his superiors, what he is ordering and what he asks, as easily as, in olden days, the shouts of the centurion. It can be imagined what coherence this procedure will bestow on operations, despite the rapid movement of men and machines.

Nevertheless, despite these facilities, the incidents of the battle must not be allowed to break the order of the attackers. After some hours, certain groups of tanks have passed the others, the infantry follows with difficulty, the artillery needs readjustment, the reinforcements have gone astray, the supplies are seeking their destination.

I

The units thus separated must be brought together again. The principal objective of the army has therefore been chosen so as to allow this regrouping. According to the type of operation, the estimated degree of resistance, and the nature of the terrain, it has been fixed at a point more or less distant from the point of departure, on an average about thirty miles away. That is, in fact, the distance necessary to be able to deploy the main body of the army, with a view to flank action against the neighbouring country, a frequent method of taking advantage of successes. That is also the depth favourable to air operations, when it is a question of detailed observations protected by fighting aircraft. The armoured units in possession of the objective reconnoitre in all directions by means of light machines in a smoke-screen. Behind this screen, infantrymen and guns occupy the conquered territory. After that, the tanks take up waiting positions towards the rear, where they get ready for fresh efforts. If there is no urgency about pushing forward, they await nightfall in order to complete their re-formation, and, in this case, until nightfall, protective clouds conceal part of the battlefield from the eyes of the enemy.

## III

But often, when success has been gained, one must make haste to gather its fruits. Leaving the objective which has been attained, the professional army will push on into the zone in which lies the spoils of war. 'Exploitation' will become a reality, whereas during the last war it was only a dream. It is true that during the recent battles, offensives, by sheer weight of men, did make a break through. In front of the attacker there opened up the road to great victories, those which, by their profound effects and rapid extension, threw the enemy into general confusion, just as the breaking of a pillar may bring down a cathedral in ruins. Those Frenchmen who, on May 9th, 1915, pushed through to Vimy, who on July 1st and 8th, 1916, pierced by a single thrust the German positions south of the Somme, and who, on August 9th, 1918, on the Ancre, completely broke the enemy ; and those Germans who, on February 23rd, 1916, before Verdun, found nothing in front of them but a dislocated defence, who on March 24th, 1918, saw the English left broken, and who ten weeks later carried the Chemin des Dames and passed Château-Thierry, could believe that the decisive hour had struck, when the advance would go on accelerating, when any bold-ness could be permitted, when the enemy was paralysed in will and would abandon himself to his fate. But these victors lacked the means of getting full value from their success. How was it possible to drive the infantry any further when they were lost, footsore, and decimated, when the guns could not follow them, nor the reinforcements catch them up, and when even orders failed to come through ? And as for the cavalry, which was incapable of crossing this shell-torn ground, badly equipped for battle, infinitely vulnerable, its dreams of a triumphal progress were shattered at the first barbed-wire entanglement commanded by machine-guns.

To-morrow, the fact of the existence of a picked body organized for pursuit will change everything. When one thinks of the weakness of ordinary formations as soon as they are attacked on the flank or in the rear, of the importance of certain vital parts of the organization and of the centralization of command, one can estimate what overwhelming effects could be obtained by the irruption of an armoured force pouring out fire in the rear of an army in modern defence grouping. The enemy's communications will be the most common objective of such manoeurves. This is an ancient precept, but it has been rejuvenated by a system of war which demands enormous equipment for the slightest skirmish, and which makes the life of armies dependent on what can be obtained from the country. The Malmaison offensive, to take only one example, required the transportation of 500,000 tons, the load of 1,000 trains or 100,000 heavy lorries. It follows that if the great road and rail arteries can be cut in several places, the fighting organism will be choked. If the *voie sacrée* had been broken, the loss of Verdun and its army would have been certain. If the German cavalry had succeeded, in September

1915, in reaching Molodetchno, the junction of the railway which saved the Russians engaged on the west of the Pripet marshes, the latter would have been faced with disaster. What utter confusion would have arisen among the German troops if the Armistice had not prevented the launching of our Lorraine offensive planned for November 14th, 1918. If the Rhine bridges, towards Coblenz and further south, had been seized in the rear of the exhausted and defeated army, what a gigantic Sedan would have made its mark in history !

In the conflicts of the future, after each break through on a front, troops will rapidly move round far in the rear of the enemy, strike at his sensitive points, throw his whole system into confusion. In this way, there will be restored that strategical extension of tactical gains which could not be obtained by Joffre or Falkenhayn, nor by Hindenburg or Foch, for lack of appropriate means, but which, in olden days, constituted the supreme end, and, as it were, the nobility of the art of war. For, if war is, in essence, destructive, the ideal of those who wage it remains, none the less, economy, the least massacre for the greatest result, a combination of forces making use of death, suffering, and terror in order to attain the goal as quickly as possible and so put an end to all three.

In addition, the aptitude for independent action, for surprise, for making the most of successes, with which the motor endows professional armies on land, will work in very well with the properties, which will in the future be essential, of fighter aircraft. It is impossible to doubt, indeed, that air squadrons,

capable of operating at a distance, possessing lightning
speed, manœuvring in three dimensions, and striking
vertical blows, which are the most impressive of all,
must play a central part in the war of the future.
But, up to now, they have lacked a complement on
the ground. For the effects produced by bombing
aircraft, terrible as they are, have something static
about them. The flying machine itself cannot draw
any advantage from its power. It is true that the ruins
it leaves in its wake, the chronic terror it produces,
have, in the long run, a serious effect on the enemy,
but these are indirect. Like artillery, of which it is,
in the final analysis, the development, aircraft can
destroy, but cannot compel, cannot conquer, cannot
occupy.

So long as there did not exist on the ground any
force capable of acting in unison with the air-fleet,
the latter had the choice of two inadequate modes
of operation. It could either limit its action to the
field within which it could help the land army, or
it could act in isolation and contribute nothing,
except indirectly, to the collective result. This was the
fate of air-bombing during the last war. It was the
same on both sides. At one time, aircraft would be
used behind the enemy front at near-by points, when
its activities fell far short of its possibilities. At other
times, it carried out raids on distant important objectives, industrial centres, ports and junctions, when it
produced great but imponderable results. From their
expeditions over Paris or Cologne, aeroplanes or
dirigibles came back, certain of having spread death
and fire ; but no advance towards the frontiers to be

crossed or the territory to be occupied followed these massacres or destructions. There was no visible correspondence between these episodes and the slow efforts of those who conquered or defended the soil— the soil which is the real object of war, since it is there that men live.

But as soon as extended raids on land became possible once more, the problem of continuity between the war in the sky and the war on land was fully and completely solved. It was possible to take immediate advantage of the material and moral destruction produced by aircraft. To throw out of order work in the Ruhr Basin by vertical bombardment will affect the total means of war at Germany's disposal, as it did before. But, in addition, an army capable of long-range enterprises will take advantage of it to rush there. The cutting of the Rhine bridges at Coblenz and at Mainz, when there is fighting round Metz, is useful, it is true, in any conditions. But what importance it would take on if guns and machine-guns were to appear on the banks of the river ! In short, there will be someone to pick up, at the foot of the tree, the fruits that fall as a result of shaking it. Inversely, the action of the aerial troops will extend that of the attackers. A fruitful path lies open for 'combined operations', which grammarians and committees to-day discuss in vain.

The last war saw the power of machinery reach an unheard-of degree, but it was brutal and unsubtle. By adding to it speed, in the hands of a select body of men, the future will restore to it some of its former character.

*"To rub the sleep out of your eyes."*—RICHEPIN.

# THE HIGH COMMAND

# I

THE CHANGES IN THE USE OF FORCE MODIFY THE training of the High Command. Not, to be sure, in its principles, for to lead men in battle, whether they are armed with a sword or are in charge of a modern tank, the task of the leader is always to weigh up the circumstances, to make decisions and to give orders and then, once the action has been launched, to reassess from time to time the system of the means at his disposal, which are continuously being modified by circumstances. Whatever the time and place, there is a sort of philosophy of command, as unchangeable as human nature, which is the true lesson of military history. When Charles XII wept at the recital of Alexander's exploits, when Bonaparte pored over Frederick the Great's campaigns, when Foch taught Napoleon's methods, it was because they were impregnated by the feeling of this permanence. To rise above oneself in order to dominate others and thereby events, is an effort which does not vary in its essentials. But its procedure does change radically.

Actually, as long as battle was no more than a muscular action of men and horses, the skill of the leader lay in keeping his forces in such a relation to the enemy, the battlefield and the sun, that their actions of cut, thrust and parry should be as far as possible efficacious and simultaneous. And since the severity of the blows struck by an army depended on its resoluteness—since fear paralyses the body and courage strengthens it—the leadership was bound to instil in its subordinates the psychological enthusiasm which increases the vigour of attack. Further, since the battle took place at short range, between men who were standing close together, every leader, even the greatest, had a direct view over the whole field of the engagement. In other words, he could give his orders without needing intermediaries and could by his presence affect the conduct of the fighters. Tactics depended on the eye, prestige on the impressions produced. Hannibal won his victories by his observations and his example.

The appearance of firearms threw the art of war, which had not changed its form since the dawn of history, into a state of chronic evolution. The development of muskets, rifles, guns has gone on constantly. But these machines were no longer simply the extension of human limbs, as the sword or the lance had been. They possessed, independent of the skill and courage of soldiers, intrinsic qualities which one had to know how to use, and they demanded services which could not be neglected. Their range, their scope, their rate of fire, and their supply, became the essential elements in the choice of formations, battlefields and times. Moreover, as intervals and distances become larger with the radius of action of weapons, and as troops found themselves forced to conceal themselves under cover, the leader, in consequence, was less easily able to see what was happening in his zone. Thus, the technical conditions relative to equipment assumed increasing importance while, on the other hand, the chief's direct action on the man who was carrying out his orders decreased from battle to battle. The best generals were those whose orders obtained the best results from firearms. Since they could not be seen by all, they set themselves to create great zeal in the ranks, and, for decisive attacks, they appeared in person at appropriate times and places. Such were Condé, Hoche, Napoleon.

Meanwhile, the last war raised to the highest point the predominance of material elements. No courage could prevail against a hail of bullets or an artillery barrage. The power acquired by weapons demanded that each enterprise should strictly conform to numerical conditions. A strict evaluation of precision, range, weight, and speed was the basis of plans. That is why the most resolute leaders, those who said "all the same" and "at all costs" were of no use whatever unless there had first been put into position a certain number of guns of a fixed calibre, supplied with so many rounds, with their method of employ laid down by timetables, range tables and calculating machines, all carefully co-ordinated. And, since all these calculations involved the collaboration of numerous specialists, the plan of battle was in fact the product of the labours of the General Staff. In addition, with rare exceptions, this bureaucracy of battle could carry through its movements at its ease, in view of the ponderousness of everything. It is true that responsibility rested solely on the leaders, and that sufficed for their merit as for their glory—but the effort of conceiving ideas was made by them less as a flash of their inspiration than as the result of the detailed proposals of their assistants. Finally, the extension of fronts and of depth, the compulsory entrenchment of combatants in the ground, and also, it has to be admitted, the attractiveness of established head-quarters, deprived the leaders, in the upper ranks, of contact with the rank-and-file. In battle, the chief's eye saw hardly anything except the map. How many thousands of men died without having seen their generals ! In short, everything combined to give the High Command a remote, collective, anonymous character, which forced into the shade genius and sensibility.

It is certain that in the future the handling of units made up of motor-vehicles will bear very deeply the impress of technique. The limits of what is possible, useful or absurd will be more rigid than ever in systems of force whose necessities are dictated by material equipment. The capabilities of machines cannot be increased, their needs cannot be reduced. The margin of imponderability which was allowed to commanders who could count on the devotion of soldiers to supplement their shortage of equipment will have to be eliminated from the reckoning hence-forward. The army of Sambre-et-Meuse marched without bread or boots, the Grand Army covered in ten days the twenty stages from Boulogne.to Mainz. To-morrow, fighting engines will stop the moment they have used their last drop of petrol and will refuse to go faster than their construction allows. On the other hand, the complexity of their organisms will demand higher and higher technical ability among those who have to look after them. It used to be said that the leader could not act efficiently without becoming part of his men. In the future, it will be said that he is worth nothing if the knowledge of what can or can not be got out of his equipment has not become second nature to him. It is true that he will not need to have in mind the detailed information which is the task of the engineer, but he will certainly need to have a feeling for mechanical combinations.

However, if the perfection of machines cannot fail to accentuate the technical character of war, at the same time, by a curious reaction, it will reintroduce into the practice of leadership certain conditions of speed and initiative which will once again restore the conspicuousness of personality. Indeed, leaders of all ranks will have to make judgments and decisions with an extreme promptitude which will exclude the possibility of councils and delays. In a few moments they will have to weigh up circumstances, come to decisions, and give their orders. No doubt, fore-thought and preparation, in order to reduce danger, will remain possible and indeed essential. But once an action has been engaged, it will most frequently take such sudden turns that the interventions of the High Command will have to be made very rapidly. There will be no more manœuvres worked out in advance, or attacks directed like a ballet, such as there were in the Great War. There will be an end to the abrupt breaking off of contact between direction and execution which zero-hour regularly brought about. There will be an end to underground dugouts, where the commander, tormented by anxiety, waited by his oil lamp while four officers co-ordinated for him doubtful information. In its place, there will be continual improvisation. The rapid improvisation of mobile units, leaders eager to see what is going on, covering the field of battle, or flying over the whole zone. In short, personal and immediate action will be established as a principle for all ranks of command.

Such a revolution in the manner of leading troops will have consequences which are not exclusively of an intellectual order. While the leader's mental task will have to follow a new rhythm, his moral effort will equally become greater and more important. In an army whose law is autonomous action, the commander will have to make a number of decisions which were spared him in the war of yesterday. It will no longer be possible to limit oneself to the literal carrying out of orders, to consult higher authority before acting, to make one's attitude conform with that of one's neighbours. Initiative, which was extolled in regulations but mistrusted in orders, will again become sovereign. Character, respected at the bottom but feared at the top, will recover all its glory on the battlefield.

Further, the reciprocal familiarity between the rank-and-file and its leaders, which the mass system impaired, will be reborn. With what could the fleeting hordes, who filled the gaps in the ranks after each slaughter, nourish their sentiments for generals whom they hardly ever saw and who sent them to their death by typewritten messages? No doubt, goodwill and discipline made certain of obedience. But between the men who, from so far away and such a height, gave the directions, and those whose bodies formed the lines and points on the maps, there was nothing to recall in the least the familiar relationship which pervaded ancient armies. There were no more hoplites eager for a glance from Alexander, legionaries dying for Caesar, veterans weeping over the body of Turenne, 'old sweats' crying "Long live the Emperor," troopers acclaiming Canrobert's plumes. This clear respect, this flame of devotion, which gave the High Command a bright halo, where are they to be found among 'the dull mass' of good cattle, of which Dragomiroff spoke? By contrast, what a position will be held among professional troops, rooted in the military order by ideals and habit, by great leaders whom they will have the opportunity and the desire to know! And, inversely, what support, perhaps even what secret compulsion, will the leaders possess in a prestige first acquired among their subordinates!

This reciprocal influence will become still more profound as the form of battle brings soldiers and generals closer together. The latter, seeking in advance the personal impressions which they will need for command, will be constantly seen by their troops. The effect of presence, which during the most gloomy of wars the most ardent of our leaders could not exert, will be restored by the motor and the flying machine. Instead of the leaders being tied to their bridgehead, as formerly—because it was the function of vital communications—they will be at the head of their troops, literally, not merely figuratively. At the same time, the dangers to be run, and the honour of their example, will increase for them. The effects which were produced on the fighting men of other days by the appearance under fire of Condé, by the golden uniform

K

of Murat, by the standard of MacMahon, will beyond doubt be reproduced at the sight of the car or the aeroplane of the commander.    And if the future casualty lists begin, as in former times, by long lists of generals, it may be so much the better for that comradeship of arms which, more than stars or stripes, remains the most noble jewel of the military crown.

## II

The value of the High Command is the final result of long and hard work. No doubt, there enters into it the variable influence of genius. No doubt there must be taken into account the more or less conscious stock of qualities and traditions accumulated by the Army. But during the few days when, twice or thrice in a century, the destiny of the people is played out on the field of battle, the judgment, the attitude, and the authority of leaders depends more than anything else on the intellectual and moral reflexes which they have acquired during their whole career.

In many periods during the past, when wars followed hard upon each other, the training of leaders was carried out by practical experience, and they were chosen by ordeal. During his whole grown-up life, Bayard only spent three years without drawing his sword. Catinat took part in twenty-eight campaigns. Davout spent twenty-three years in fighting. What need was there in these conditions to organize the instruction of future generals? War itself took charge of the matter, as it also showed up the deserving and provided them with favourable opportunities for proving their merit. A training so empirical might lead, at times, to that inactivity of mind which is the result of over-addiction to a profession. The generals might perhaps have been more efficient if they had been occasionally relieved from the immediate demands of their office, and had worked out in general terms the many lessons which they picked up piecemeal. But what of it? Action, a jealous mistress, absorbed their zeal and consumed their leisure!

In our time, war has become so huge that only rarely do nations have recourse to it. On the other hand, radical differences distinguish each conflict from its predecessor. In other words, in the period between two trials of strength the leaders lack the test of experience in their work and they are not chosen for the results they have achieved in battles. But since it is none the less necessary that they should be trained and should be distinguished in their profession, theory has to provide the lessons and guide their selection. That is where the danger begins. It is true that the foresight of a Moltke created, in peace-time, a General Staff perfectly capable of carrying out the task which awaited it. Nor can one deny that before 1914 France had prepared a High Command of real value. This does not disprove the fact that normally, during the years of theoretical work without practical application, a thousand unfavourable influences lead the heads of the Army astray. And thus it is that early battles are full of mistakes in leadership and bring into the lime-light qualities and defects that have remained concealed until then.

It is true that the Army of to-day, having, during the last war, gauged the capabilities of the High Command and realized the cost of inefficiency, carries out a tremendous professional labour in all its branches. Besides the schools properly so-called, there are innumerable course of lectures, terms of probation, centres, cycles, instructional periods, which periodically bring together officers of all ranks. The training of cadres is being carried out more and more. It is impossible to keep count of the committees for study and research. The military career is the only one which imposes on its members, from the highest to the lowest, the task of perpetually improving its acquired knowledge. And the astonished public sees generals grown old in the Service hurrying off to lectures, clutching under their arms the paraphernalia of the student. Yet, if one considers the basis of this activity, one realizes that anxiety for the future does yield somewhat to respect for the past. The military caste, which has absorbed some terrible lessons, seems to have a tendency to give its chosen leaders the training designed for action in circumstances similar to those through which it has just passed. A great deal of labour aims at training every man to play his part in a centralized system and to conform to rigid rules, the whole thing codified in accordance with the model of the events of 1918. Certainly, this produces remarkable unity and many good qualities. But the renewal of doctrines as methods of making war change, and the inclination of ideas to follow the evolution of things—which have brought about victories in every age—find conditions far from favourable in this rigidity.

It is striking to note that the periods of history, in which the High Command, taken as a whole, gave proof of the highest qualities, have also been those in which the purely didactic order of things exercised the least influence on it. The great generals of antiquity, who tell us of their exploits, never refer to any lessons they have received. In the Anabasis of Xenophon, or the Commentaries of Caesar, there is not the least allusion to principles, but only the description of cirstances and decisions. Whence did Gustavus-Adolphus, Prince Eugene, Luxembourg and Maurice of Saxony draw their inspiration if not from their own talent? The constellation of generals who achieved so many successes during the Revolution and the Empire did not even possess standing orders. It is a remarkable fact that those leaders in the Great War who showed the greatest capability had, in earlier days, evinced notorious independence of official doctrines. No doubt, all of them possessed a knowledge of the means at their disposal and also the ability to fall back on intuition which comes from experience. But the creative spark, which continually flashed forth, did not come to them from a code. They owed the genesis of their actions to themselves alone.

In order to prepare commanders to lead troops completely different from the heavy masses of the Great War, a change must be made in the method of training leaders. This method, instead of drawing its inspiration chiefly from the acquired knowledge systematized in a body of doctrine by well-supervised professional lecturers, will have to take the development of personality for its law. This does not mean, of course, that training must encourage recklessness or exalt arbitrariness. Military action, whatever its form, consists in the first place of the study of the elements of the problem, and this requires a discipline of mind which excludes fantasy. In addition, the means at disposal have fixed properties, respect for which in their case is an inflexible condition. Finally, every

warlike undertaking proceeds from a mission which is
not chosen and cannot be discussed. But the syntheses
which follows this analysis, instead of being suggested
by *a priori* criteria, should be sought by the leader
nowhere but within himself. To exercise imagination,
judgment, and decision, not in a certain direction, but
for their own sake and with no other aim than to make
them strong and free, will be the philosophy of the
training of leaders.

At the same time, in spite of possessing depth of
reflection, competence in synthesis, and sureness of
judgment, without which professional knowledge
would be worthless, those who have the germ of
leadership would develop it badly if they applied
themselves solely to military subjects. Power of mind
implies a versatility that one does not obtain through
exclusive practice of one's profession, for the same
reason that one finds it difficult to entertain oneself in
the bosom of one's family. The real school of leadership is therefore general culture. Through it the mind
learns to act in orderly fashion, to distinguish the
essential from the trivial, to recognize developments
and causes of interference, in short, to educate itself
to a level where the whole can be appreciated without
prejudice to the shades of difference within it. There
has been no illustrious captain who did not possess
taste and a feeling for the heritage of the human mind.
At the root of Alexander's victories one will always
find Aristotle.

Men, however, in the army as elsewhere, are not
fashioned solely by training. Life sets its mark upon
them. To take the initiative in action would be

completely meaningless, if the whole of military existence tended to sterilize it. It must be agreed that the system of leadership and administration applied to the troops and services does not conduce to autonomous action. A crushing centralization weighs on the whole and on its component parts. Countless text books continually added to, modified, and revised, keep every rank, up to the highest, in narrow leading-strings. A mass of undergrowth wherein to take cover, entrenchment against responsibility, are not only open to, but imposed upon, leaders of all ranks. If it is officially proclaimed that they are expected to produce results, then in fact, what is demanded is the strict observation of the regulations in force. But, by becoming too complicated, the law becomes self-contradictory. No human power could satisfy at once all the prescriptions of the various regulations. That is why authority, whose demands stifle free action, is not even able to act as a protection. And, while it crushes enthusiasm and emasculates character, it loses its prestige little by little through excessive intervention.

No doubt, a mass military system can, if necessary, accommodate itself to the vigour of such an organization. If one is dealing with a formless mass summarily and provisionally, this levelling to mediocrity is, after all, supportable. But a professional army, designed for rapid action, needs a different leaven. In order to secure distinguishing characteristics for military formations, the leaders must stamp their own images on them. They must be allowed the right to do that. To fix the aim to be achieved, to excite the spirit of emulation, and to judge the results, is the task of

superior authority with regard to each unit. But as
to the manner of doing it, let each man be master in
his own house ! The only route which will lead to
the spirit of enterprise is decentralization.

Whatever may be the effect, on the value of leaders,
of more liberal training and wider autonomy, the essential thing will remain, as always, the personal hidden
efforts of those who aspire to command. For, if the
imparting of instruction and daily routine suffice to
fashion most of our fellow-creatures, the more powerful
of them form themselves. Destined to leave their
impress, rather than to receive one, they build up in
the secrecy of their inner life the structure of their
feelings, of their ideas, of their will. That is why, in
the tragic hours when the storm sweeps away conven-
tions and customs, they alone stand up, and are therefore necessary. Nothing is of more importance to the
State than to produce in its reserve of officers these
exceptional men who will be its final resource.

But the strain of existence involved by such preparation carries with it in ordinary times small rewards
and great trials. The depth, the singularity, the self-
sufficiency of a man made for great deeds is not
popular except in critical times. Although when in
contact with him one is conscious of a superiority
which compels respect, he is seldom liked. Moreover,
his faculties, shaped for heroic feats, despise the
pliability, the intrigues and the parade through which
most brilliant careers are achieved in peace time. And
so he would be condemned to emasculation or cor-
ruption, if he lacked the grim impulse of ambition to
spur him on. It is not, to be sure, that the passion for

rank and honours, which is only careerism, possess him, but it is, beyond doubt, the hope of playing a great rôle in great events !

This, moreover, is one of the reasons which make it necessary that soldiers should be convinced of their warlike future. A picked military force which did not live in the desire of battle would soon fall into decadence. The single idea of revenge was sufficient to keep alive the zeal of our officers for forty years. Whatever may be the ends which are aimed at in the outside world, it would be extremely impolitic for the State not to maintain in the Army the idea of a great task to be carried out and a desire for vast enterprises. Failing that, when the day of danger comes, the Motherland will seek in vain for men worthy of victory.

For Glory gives herself only to those who have always dreamed of her.

# III

The creation of a properly-equipped army of volunteers, however necessary and in harmony with the tendency of evolution it may be, nevertheless represents a reform of very broad scope. Established ideas will be modified by it, like the policy and the technique of war. In the history of the French Army there are only at the most four or five upheavals comparable to it in scope and consequences. Such a refashioning will be painful for the military body, and it cannot be expected of it if it is not organized by powerful authority.

For the Army, by its very nature, resists change. This does not mean, of course, that the sense of progress is lacking among those who serve it. It would be easy to prove that, of all institutions, the Army provides the richest collection of men of thought, of science, and of action. But this broadness of mind among individuals does preclude collective cautiousness. Since it lives by stability, by conformity, by tradition, the Army instinctively fears anything that tends to modify its structure. In addition, a strict hierarchy waters down such projects. Finally, the vagaries of peacetime create, as between departments in which decisions are made, rivalries and jealousies which create opposition to the disturbance of equilibrium. It has to be added, incidentally, that this prudence is in some measure justified by attacks delivered from outside. The military code of the country, on account of the expenditure it involves, its inevitable unpopularity, and its characteristic of answering to future and deferred needs, is a chosen object of attack by politicians bidding for popular favour. Since the innovations proposed under cover of noisy rhetoric usually have a weakening effect, it is only too easy to understand the mistrust of the men who have to deal with it. For these men, who can be described as 'experts', are kept at a distance and subjected to abuse while measures of preparation are being discussed, but find themselves none the less responsible for the warlike events which are the consequence. The whole world knows the name of the leader who was unlucky in the attack on the frontiers and afterwards victorious on the Marne. But who could list the numerous ministers, journalists, theoreticians, orators and publicists, whose ephermeral acts were scattered in a thousand meetings, documents and discussion, and covered by practically anonymous votes and were yet of so much importance for the overhauling of and for filling the gaps in our military system ?

Various reasons, then, some permanent and some accidental, make the Army feel apprehensive with regard to great reforms. As a consequence, such reforms are never, in the ordinary way, put into effect through the initiative of the organization itself. The chronicles tell us of the anger of the old bands which were broken up by Charles VII to make way for permanent troops. When Louvois created the regular army, he had to overcome much opposition from the reserve of officers. The joint system which Carnot imposed at first pleased neither the troops of the line nor the volunteers. The system of 1818, due to Gouvion-Saint-Cyr, received little support from the soldiers of the Empire. In 1867, the plan of Marshal Niel, who aimed at forming reserves, met with opposition from the Military Commission. It was Monsieur Thiers, in person, who presided over the reorganization of 1872.

In order to bring into being the professional army, and in order that that army should be provided with the material and with the new spirit without which it will never be more than a will-o'-the-wisp, a leader will have to appear whose judgment is independent, whose orders are irresistible, and who is well thought of by public opinion. He must be in the service of only the State, free from prejudices, disdaining patronage. He must be firmly committed to his task, absorbed in far-reaching plans, well-informed about the men and things to be dealt with. He must be a leader who is at one with the army, devoted to those he commands, eager for responsibility ; a man strong enough to compel, clever enough to persuade and great enough to carry through a great task. Such will be the minister, soldier or politician, to whom the nation will owe the next reconstruction of its forces.

If one looks only at appearances, one might think, it is true, that the conditions in which the State functions to-day allow no one the authority or the time to carry through such an undertaking. There are so many dissensions and so many contingencies in public life that the best activities, even when they are set in motion, seldom lead to results. But this very paralysis creates the desire for a cure in our old world.

Between the fervours of the social system and the sclerosis of power, opposition is too flagrant. Our generation, so anxious for results—horsepower, records, series, specialists, cost price : our age, so eager for clarity—naked lights, healthy straight lives, women in bathing costumes, Véritas offices ; our century leaning towards displays of force—competitions, cartels, picked men, propaganda, nationalism ; these will no longer accept the slowness, confusion and weakness that easier times were willing to bear. For a thousand reasons, indeed, a change must come. These is no doubt that in a short while, resolute people will be able to open up the paths of conquest by bending existing institutions to new ideas.

If this national reforging has to begin with the army, that is perfectly in conformity with the natural order of things. This is not only because force is more necessary than ever for nations that want to survive, but also because the military body is the most complete expression of the spirit of a social system. It is by the history of its legions that Rome is best understood. The royal troops were the mirror of our old monarchy. Who can think of the Revolution without conjuring up the Volunteers ? In the hard task of restoring France's youth, the new army will serve as remedy and leaven. For the sword is the axis of the world, and greatness cannot be shared.

# HUTCHINSON
# &
# ASSOCIATED COMPANIES

## Famous Cheap Editions 4/-, 3/6, 3/-

### (Fiction Only)

(B) HURST & BLACKETT    (J) JARROLD    (P) STANLEY PAUL    (L) JOHN LONG
(S) SKEFFINGTON    (SB) SELWYN & BLOUNT    (M) MELROSE    (H) HUTCHINSON

## 4/- Net

BILEAU, ETHEL
When Yellow Leaves   (H)
Turnip Tops
Hippy Buchan
Arches of the Years
Box Of Spikenard
Fire of Spring
Clansmen
Ballade in G Minor

FRANKAU, GILBERT
Secret Services   (H)
Experiments in Crime
Dangerous Years
Farewell Romance
Three Englishmen
Masterson
Concerning Peter Jackson and Others
Everywoman
Life—And Erica
Martin Make Believe
Men, Maids and Mustard-Pot
Seeds of Enchantment
So Much Good
Lonely Man
Love Story of Aliette Brunton
Wine, Women and Waiters
Women of the Horizon
More of Us
Gerald Cranston's Lady
Christopher Strong
Twelve Tales
Peter Jackson

GIBBS, PHILIP
*This Nettle, Danger   (H)
Blood Relations
Cities of Refuge
Paradise for Sale
Master of Life
Darkened Rooms
Heirs Apparent   (H)
Helen of Lancaster Gate
Cross of Peace
The Golden Years
The Hidden City
The Street of Adventure
The Winding Lane

GIBBS, PHILIP—(contd.)
Young Anarchy
The Middle of the Road
Great Argument

HEPPLE, ANNE
Touch Me Not   (H)
And Then Came Spring
Untempered Wind
Run Away Family
The Old Woman Speaks
Gay Go Up
Jemima Rides
Ask Me No More
Riders of the Sea
Susan Takes a Hand
*Evening at the Farm

JACOB, NAOMI
This Porcelain Clay   (H)
Fade Out
Timepiece
Barren Metal
Founder of the House
Honour Come Back
Four Generations
Groping
Poor Straws
Props
Young Emmanuel
Roots
Seen Unknown
That Wild Lie
The Loaded Stick
The Lenient God
No Easy Way
Straws in Amber

MUSKETT, NETTA
*To-day Is Ours   (H)
Mirror For Dreams
After Rain
Jade Spider
Nor Any Dawn
The Flickering Lamp
The Open Window
Shallow Cup
Silver Gilt
Tamarisk
Wings in the Dust
Painted Heaven

MUSKETT, NETTA—(contd.)
Middle Mist
Shadow Market
Blue Haze
Ally Cat
Misadventure
The Plaster Cast

SABATINI, RAFAEL
The Fortunes of Captain Blood   (H)
The Romantic Prince
Anthony Wilding
Bellarion
Chivalry
Fortune's Fool
Love at Arms
Scaramouche
Scaramouche the King-maker
Banner of the Bull
Black Swan
Hounds of God
The Minion
The Sea Hawk
The Snare
The Stalking Horse
The Tavern Knight
Venetian Masque
Chronicles of Captain Blood
The Marriage of Corbal (Film edition)
The Lost King
The Strolling Saint   (P)
The Lion's Skin

WHEATLEY, DENNIS
The Quest of Julian Day(H)
Contraband
Secret War
They Found Atlantis
Eunuch of Stamboul
The Devil Rides Out
Fabulous Valley
The Forbidden Territory
Such Power is Dangerous
Black August
Uncharted Seas
The Golden Spaniard
*Sixty Days to Live

* New titles

* New titles

2

BO

* New titles

* New titles

* New titles

5

HAMILTON, COSMO—(*contd.*)
Another Scandal (*B*)
Laughing Mask
Undelivered Letters
Scandal
*Thy Lamp O'Memory (*H*)
Adam and Evelyn
Splender of Torches
Pinnion
The Armour of Light
Drama Within Drama
HAMILTON, HARRY
Banjo on my Knee (*B*)
All Their Children Were
Acrobats
HANDLEY, LEONARD
*Remote Journey (*L*)
HANNA, EVELYN
*Blackberry Winter (*H*)
HARCOURT, J. M.
It Never Fails (*L*)
HARDING, ANTHONY
Arms for the Love of Allah
(*H*)
HARDING, REVEL
Wild Balm (*S*)
Rooks Build Low
HARDWICK, BERNARD
Sinners at the Manse (*L*)
Honour Thy Father
HARSANYI, ZSOLT
Hungarian Melody (*B*)
HARTHERN, ERNST
Home at Last (*J*)
HASLETT, G. WYNDHAM
Portrait on the Shadows
(*B*)
HEATH, MAUDE
Herb O'Grace (*B*)
HEDWORTH, BARBARA
The Woman Yonder (*J*)
The Woman in Possession
Through the Front Door
Give me the Man
Foolish Pelican
You Can't Trust Men
No Escape
HELIER, MONIQUE St.
The Abandoned Wood (*S B*)
HELLAND, LEWIS
Cairo Caprice (*J L*)
HENRY, HARRIET
The Lady With a Past (*P*)
The Rakish Halo
Touch Us Gently
HERITAGE, A. J.
Happy Years (*H*)
HERVEY, HARRY
*The Damned Don't Cry (*L*)
HEWITT, E. L.
Dangerous Edge (*H*)
HEWITT, KATHLEEN
Mardi (*J*)
Pattern in Yellow (*J*)
Go Find a Shadow
Golden Milestone
HEWLETT, DOROTHY
Victorian House (*B*)
HILMAR, ARTHUR J.
Erica, My Daughter (*J*)
HITCHENS, ROBERT
Secret Information (*B*)
HOGARTH, MARJORIE
The Eyes of a Fool (*H*)
HOPE, FIELDING
The Guinea Pig's Tail (*S B*)

HORT, G. M.
The Peace Fire (*M*)
HUGHES, RUPERT
Man Without a Home (*J*)
True Lover's Knot
No One Man
Double Exposure
HUNT, DOROTHY
Reflections (*B*)
HUNT, VIOLET
Their Hearts (*P*)
The Last Ditch
The Doll
HYDE, ROBIN
Wednesday's Children (*B*)
The Godwits Fly
Nor the Years Condemn
Thee
Check to your King
Passport to Hell
ILES, FRANCIS
As For the Woman (*J*)
INGRAM, GEORGE
Stir (*M*)
JAMES, NORAH C.
By a Side Wind (*J*)
JEANS, ANGELA
The Field Beyond (*L*)
JEPSON, EDGAR
The Sweepstake Winner (*J*)
JONES, IDWELL
Whistler Van (*S B*)
JORGENSEN, NELS LEROY
Laughing Cabellero (*M*)
JULIAN, MARY
Lucifer's Court (*P*)
The Wedding Guest
KANTOR, MACKINLAY
The Voice of Bugle Ann (*S*)
KEEPING, JAMES
The Days Before (*L*)
KENNEDY, JOAN
Yesterday's Roses (*H*)
According to Judy
Background for Barbara
Blue of Beyond
Deep Furrows
Miss Lavender of London
Green Harvest
Of That Red Soil
Punchinello
Ragged Orchid
The Splendid Snare
Earthenware
Community House
A Torch on Women
Time's Fool
To-morrow Comes
*Mimosa Dust
KNIGHT, KOBOLD
Peter Called Simon and
Other Stories (First time
published) (*H*)
KNITTEL, JOHN
The Asp and Other Stories
(*H*)
Nile Gold
Inter The Abyss
Via Mala
Doctor Abrahim (3/-)
KRASSNOFF, PETER
NICHOLAEVITCH
Largo (*H*)
LANCASTER, VICKY
*Daughter at Home (*B*)

LANCING, GEORGE
Fraudulent Conversion (*P*)
Peking Glass
LANDELS, D. H.
Jane and Saturday (*P*)
LANDI, ELISSA
The Ancestor (*B*)
LANE, TEMPLE
The Trains Go South (*J*)
LANGMAID, MARGARET
Precious Burden (*H*)
Related by Marriage
LANGTON, JOY
Blind Arrows (*H*)
LAWFORD, FLORENCE
Bridge of Hope (*P*)
Suzette
The Kindly Vision
Leaves Before the Wind
Merryheart
LAWRENCE, MARGERY
Terraces of Night (*B*)
Silken Sarah
The Madonna of Seven
Moons
The Drums of Youth
Bohemian Glass
The Crooked Smile (*J*)
Madam Holle
The Floating Café
Overture to Life
Red Heels (*H*)
LEA, FANNY HEASLIP
Happy Landings (*J*)
Good-bye Summer
LEE, DORCAS
The Offending Adam (*L*)
LESLIE, DORIS
*Another Cynthia (*H*)
The Starling (*B*)
LESLIE, HENRIETTA
Daughters Defiant (*J*)
Mother of Five (*J*)
LESLIE, SHANE
Fifteen Odd Stories (*H*)
LEWIS, HELEN
PROTHERO
The Peep Show (*H*)
As God Made Her
LEWIS, HILDA
Madam Gold (*B*)
Pegasus Yoked
Full Circle
Because I Must (*J*)
LONG, ETHEL
Hollywood Masque (*L*)
LORIMER, NORMA
A Wife Out of Egypt (*P*)
On Etna
LORNE, JOAN
Foolish Saint (*P*)
London Lady
LOWNDES, MRS. BELLOC
Motive (*H*)
Injured Lover
And Call It Accident
McCLEOD, PRISCILLA
Turn Back The Pages (*L*)
MACDONNELL, O. S.
Thorston Hall (*S B*)
George Ashbury
MACHEN, ARTHUR
The Children of the Pool
and Other Stories (*H*)
MACKENZIE, COMPTON
Seven Ages of Women (*H*)

* New titles

6

* New titles

* New titles

* New titles

9

## Mystery and Detection

* New titles

* New titles

* New titles

* New titles

## Historical

BOWEN, MARJORIE
  A Giant in Chains   (H)
  God and the Wedding Dress
  Trumpets at Rome

BROWNE, DOUGLAS G.
  The House of the Sword (H)

BUCHANAN, VINCENT
  One Door Shuts   (B)

CHAIR, SOMERSET de
  Enter Napoleon   (H)

DRURY, LIEUT. COL. W.P.
  *"Fightincocks"   (H)

DUFFUS, R. L.
  Jornada   (H)

DURYCH, J.
  The Descent of the Idol (H)

GOUTH, GEORGE W.
  A Daughter of Kings  (S)

HARDY, ARTHUR
  The Splendid Adventurer
      (H)

KESTEN, HERMANN
  Spanish Fire   (H)

LESLIE, S. B.
  *Charleston Bound  (B)

LINDSAY, PHILIP
  Bride for a Buchaneer (H)
  Nutbrown Maid

MAPPLE, NELSON
  The Haunted Suit  (B)

MASON, G. M.
  Gay Valiance   (H)

NEUMANN, ALFRED
  Man of December  (H)

RAY, J. FLETCHER
  The Hand That Drove The
  Nails   (S)

RYLAND, CLIVE
  Romantic Heart   (H)

SALVERSON, LAURA
  GOODMAN
  Black Lace   (H)

SARASIN, J. G.
  The Caspian Song  (H)
  Stars Above Paris
  Revolt in the Palace

SHANNON, KITTY
  High Toby   (H)
  Venus in Trousers
  Jean de Batz

TAYLOR, W. F.
  Beau Rogue   (L)

TIMMS, E. V.
  Alicia Deane   (S)
  The Cripple in Black
  Whitehall
  Far Caravan   (H)

VOCE, ANTON
  Royal Purple   (H)

## Humour

ATTIWELL, KEN
  Sky Steward   (L)

BOON, FRANCIS
  Ancient and Fishlike (L)

BOYLE, C. NINA
  Good old Potts   (P)

BUTLER, JOAN
  *Happy Christmas  (P)
  Half Shot
  Team Work
  Trouble Brewing
  Monkey Business
  Unnatural Hazards
  The Light Lover
  The Heavy Husband
  Something Rich
  Half Holiday
  Rapid Fire

DEWES, SIMON
  *Reluctant Revelry  (J)

GILBEY, GEOFFREY
  Not Really Rude  (L)

GODBER, NOËL
  Don't Do It, Doctor ! (L)
  Amazing Spectacles
  Keep it Dark
  How Dare You, Sir !
  Twin Bedsteads
  Miss Barelegs

HELLAND, LEWIS
  Cairo Caprice   (L)

JAMES, JAMES
  Guide Book to Women (B)

KEIGHTLEY, J. W.
  Near The Shrimp's Whis-
  kers   (P)
  The Splinter in the Water-
  Chute

KILPATRICK, FLORENCE
  What a Liberty   (L)

MAPPLE, NELSON
  Bye, Bye Blackbeard (B)
  Highly Explosive

PYE, RODNEY
  He Had to See Susie (L)

WOODMAN, G. D.
  The Runaway Lover (B)
  Tony Maloney

## Adventure

ALAN, A. J.
  Good Evening, Everyone
      (H)

BENNETT, JAMES
  Chinese Blake   (S)

BETTANY, GEORGE
  The Black Horseman (S)
  The Valley of Echoes
  The Secret of the Swamp
  Villainy
  Scarbrow

BLAKE, SNGWDON
  Something About a Sailor
      (P)
  Next Port Eldorado

BRAND, ADAM
  White Sun   (H)

CHANNING, MARK
  The White Python  (H)
  King Cobra
  The Poisoned Mountain
  Indian Village

CHATTERTON, E.
  KEBLE
  Below the Surface  (B)
  Sea Spy
  Secret Ship

COE, CHARLES FRANCES
  Knockout   (H)

COXON, F. GEORGE
  Till Hell Freezes  (P)

CRAIG, THURLOW
  Love Under Smoke  (H)

* New titles

14

CUNNINGHAM, WM.
Tough Guy                    (L)

CUTCLIFFE-HYNE, C. J.
McTod                        (H)
The Rev. Captain Kettle

DELMONT, JOSEPH
Fraulein Bandit              (H)

DELVES-BROUGHTON, J.
*The Siege                   (H)

DODGE, LOUIS
Wagon Ruts                   (H)

ELLSBERG, COMMANDER
EDWARD
Submerged (An Epic of
Submarine Service)           (B)

EX-LEGIONNAIRE 1384
Soulless Legion              (B)

FERGUSON, W. B. M.
Wyoming Tragedy              (L)
Lightnin' Calvert
The Reckoning
The Singing Snake
The Island of Surprises
The Vanishing Men
Crackerjack
Somewhere Off Borneo
Bobo Marches
Dog Fox

FORAN, ROBERT W.
Land of Fear                 (H)

FRANCIS, GRANT R.
Blood Feud                   (H)

GOULD, NAT
The Racing Adventures of
Barry Bromley                (L)
Trainers' Tales

HALES, A. G.
As An Eagle Swoops           (L)
Gore of the Guides
Anber Crane's Vengeance
McGlusky the Mormon
McGlusky in India
McGlusky O' the Legion
McGlusky The Sea Rover
Devil May Care
Joy Beaucarnis
As a Woman Sows
Red Hawk

HILL, HERBERT
Retreat from Death           (H)

HULL, E. M.
The Forest of Terrible
Things                       (H)

HYDE, ROBIN
Check to your King           (B)
Passport to Hell

KROGER, THEODORE
The Forgotten Village        (H)

MEADOWS, DENIS
Italian Red                  (L)

MUNDY, TALBOT
The Purple Pirate            (H)
Jungle Jest
W. H.
Woman of Ayisha
C.I.D.
Jimgrim
Jimgrim and Allah's Peace
Om.
Gunga Sahib
The Hundred Days
The Marriage of Meldrum
Strange
Caesar Dies
The Seventeen Thieves of
El-Kalil
*The Valient View

PENNY, F. E.
A Spell of the Devil         (H)

POLLARD, CAPTAIN A. O.
Cipher Five                  (H)

"RAJPUT"
Khyber Calling               (B)

SCOGGINS, C. E.
The House of Dawn            (S)

"SEAWRACK"
Sea Trails                   (H)

SETON, GRAHAM
Pelican Row                  (H)
An Eye for An Eye
Minos Magnificent
The Viper of Luxor
Blood Money

"SINBAD"
Fathomless                   (P)
Seaworthy
The Silver Ship
Tares
Old Glory
Adrift
Nita of Martinique
Nor Breed Nor Birth

SMITH, W. H.
Red Ivory                    (S)

SNELL, EDMUND
Yellow Jacket                (S)

SOUTAR, ANDREW
The Chosen of the Gods       (J)
In the Blood

STACPOOLE, H. DE VERE
Ginger Adams                 (H)
The Sunstone
Green Coral (Stories)
City in the Sea
The Longshore Girl
Mandarin Gardens
Ocean Tramps
The Chank Shell
High Yaller
Old Sailors Never Lie
Due East of Friday

STEELE, V. M.
Hunters of Humans            (P)
Beloved of Ishmael
The Scarred Wrists

STONEHAM, C. T.
Elephant Brother             (H)

"TANJONG"
The Scarlet Bee              (H)

TAYLOR, W. F.
Barbado                      (L)
Beau Rogue

TRACY, LOUIS
The Captain of the Kansas
(J)

TURNBULL, PATRICK
Dusty Shoes                  (B)

VAN HORN, CHARLES
The Quest of Krang           (H)

VOLK, GORDON
In Brighton Waters           (S)
The Zoo Ship
Bamboo Bay
Devil's Whirlpool
The Green Ship
Isle of Men
The Lighthouse Mystery
Sea Cave
South of the Line
Tideless Sea

WEBSTER, F. A. M.
Son of Abdan                 (H)
Star Lady
Lord of the Leopards

WIGNALL, TREVOR
*Sea Green                   (H)

WILSON, GROVE
The Monster of Snowden
Hall                         (S)

# 3/- Novels

## *Western*

AMES, JOSEPH B.
The Stranger from
Cheyenne                     (H)
Louden from Larami
Man from Painted Post
Lone Hand Larrigan

AMES, JOSEPH B.—(*contd.*)
Valley of Missing Men
Shoebar Stratton

BALLEW, CHARLES
The Gambler of Red
Gulch                        (L)

BALLEW, CHARLES—(*contd.*)
From Rag Town to Ruby
Red Gold

BARRINGTON, G. W.
Bandits of Bald Hill         (H)
Red of Circle G.

* New titles